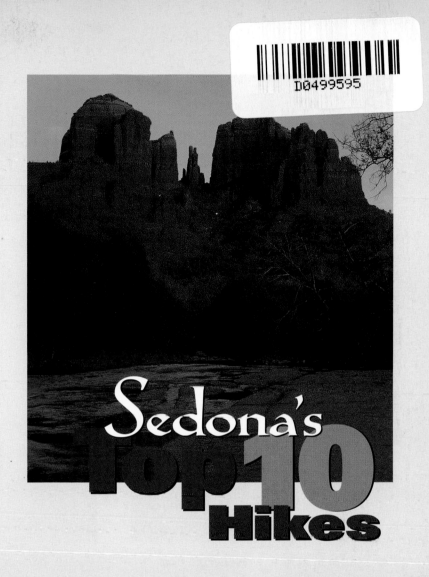

Sedona's Top10 Hikes

by Dennis Andres

photography by
Larry Lindahl

map illustrations by
Bronze Black

Published by
Meta Adventures Publishing
90 East Big Horn Court
Sedona, AZ 86351
www.MrSedona.com
info@MrSedona.com

3rd printing - 2007

Photos: ©2004 Larry Lindahl
Maps: ©2004 Bronze Black
Book design: Larry Lindahl
GPS data: Alvin Derouen

For information on books:
Dreams In Action
Distribution and Publishing
P.O. Box 1894
Sedona, AZ 86339
928-204-1560
www.DreamsInAction.us
info@DreamsInAction.us

For information on tours:
Sedona Private Guides
A division of Meta Adventures
928-204-2201
www.MrSedona.com
www.SedonaPrivateGuides.com
info@SedonaPrivateGuides.com

Thanks to Dee Glillespie, Pamela
and John Chionis, Ben Jayston,
John True, Nancy Andres, Kathleen
Bryant, Kathrine Burnham, and the
Sedona Historical Society.

Praise to those who walk and protect
these trails including Friends of the
Forest, Sedona Westerners, Yavapai
County Search and Rescue, and
U.S. Forest Service.

ISBN-13: 978-0972-1202-2-7
ISBN-10: 9721202-2-X
SAN: 254-6183

Library of Congress,
Control Number: 2004106108

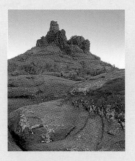

Bell Rock
Easy/Short
A gentle hike around
a famous formation
1-2 hours
Up to 4 mi. roundtrip
Village of Oak Creek
pg. 15

Cathedral
Easy/Short
Along Oak Creek to
a magnificent view
30 to 40 min.
Up to 1.5 miles
West Sedona
pg. 25

Doe Mesa
Moderate/Short
Zig-zag your way to
spectacular views
1 hour, 30 min.
2.5 miles roundtrip
West Sedona
pg. 57

Brins Mesa
Moderate/Longer
A great ramble that will
make you glad you came
3 hours, 25 min.
5 miles roundtrip
Uptown Sedona
pg. 67

TABLE OF CONTENTS

West Fork
Easy/Longer
A romantic walk
spring through fall
Up to 3 hours, 30 min.
6.4 miles roundtrip
Oak Creek Canyon
pg. 33

Boynton
Easy/Longer
Touch the sacred in
this deep red canyon
3 hours, 30 min.
6.3 miles roundtrip
West Sedona
pg. 43

Devil's Bridge
Moderate/Short
A short jaunt to a
geological wonder
1 hour, 10 min.
2 miles roundtrip
West Sedona
pg. 51

Huckaby
Moderate/Longer
A roller-coaster trail
with thrilling views
3 hours
4.9 miles roundtrip
Uptown Sedona
pg. 79

Munds Wgn
Strenuous/Longer
Rise above the red rocks
on this great new trail
4 hours, 25 min.
8 miles roundtrip
Uptown Sedona
pg. 89

Bear Mtn
Strenuous/Longer
The best big climb
for over-achievers
5-6 hours
5 miles roundtrip
West Sedona
pg. 99

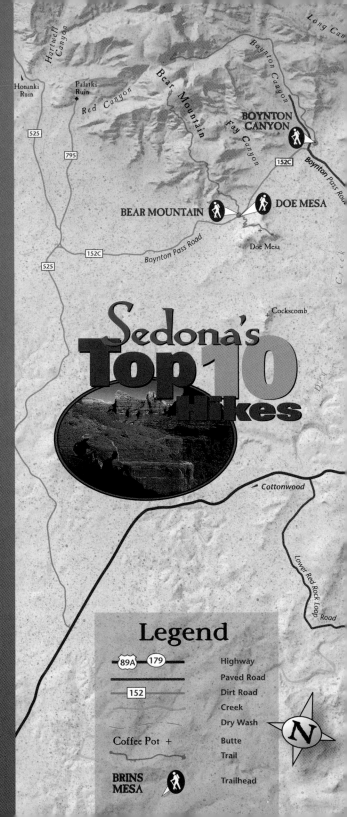

DRIVE TIMES

"Y" 89A/179 intersection
VOC Village of Oak Creek
✳ Vortex area

BELL/COURTHOUSE ✳
Village of Oak Creek area
from the "Y": 11 minutes
from VOC: 1 minute

CATHEDRAL ROCK ✳
West Sedona area
from the "Y": 13 minutes
from VOC: 13 minutes

WEST FORK
Oak Creek Canyon area
from the "Y": 23 minutes
from VOC: 34 minutes

BOYNTON CANYON ✳
West Sedona area
from the "Y": 15 minutes
from VOC: 26 minutes

DEVILS BRIDGE
West Sedona area
from the "Y": 14 minutes
from VOC: 26 minutes

DOE MESA
West Sedona area
from the "Y": 21 minutes
from VOC: 32 minutes

BRINS MESA
Uptown Sedona area
from the "Y": 6 minutes
from VOC: 17 minutes

HUCKABY
Uptown Sedona area
from the "Y": 3 minutes
from VOC: 13 minutes

MUNDS WAGON ✳
Uptown Sedona area
from the "Y": 3 minutes
from VOC: 13 minutes

BEAR MOUNTAIN
West Sedona area
from the "Y": 21 minutes
from VOC: 32 minutes

Sedona's Top 10 Hikes

Long Can
Hartwell Canyon
Boynton Canyon
Bear Mountain
Red Canyon
Palatki Ruin
Honanki Ruin
Fay Canyon

BOYNTON CANYON

525
795
152C
Boynton Pass Road

BEAR MOUNTAIN   **DOE MESA**

Doe Mesa

152C
525
Boynton Pass Road
Creek

Cockscomb

Dry

Cottonwood

Lower Red Rock Loop Road

Legend

89A / 179 — Highway
─────── Paved Road
152 Dirt Road
Creek
Dry Wash
Coffee Pot + Butte
Trail
BRINS MESA 🥾 Trailhead

N

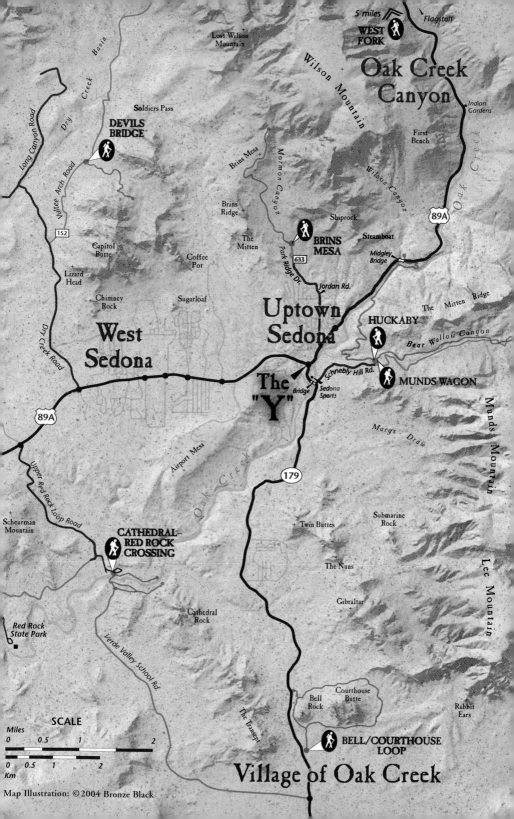

Introduction

You should expect
something special when
you walk in Sedona.

Welcome to Sedona, Arizona, an absolutely fantastic place to go for a walk in nature. I am always hopeful, as a local resident and professional guide, that people will see more of Red Rock Country, rather than less.

I learned what it means to be dedicated to the client's happiness and success while hiking with the Sherpas in Nepal. *Sedona's Top Ten Hikes* differs from other hike books in this respect. As a Sedona resident, I've taken the perspective of your local, up-to-date, personal guide. Everything about this book is designed with your comfort and enjoyment in mind.

No matter how much or little time you've been in the outdoors, my goal is to help you connect with nature—from a gentle walk along Oak Creek to the hearty adventure up Bear Mountain. Rather than just ten trails, this book offers you ten unique Sedona outings, each with interesting and useful information only an insider would know.

HOW TO USE THIS BOOK

Choosing a Hike

Assessing which trail to take may involve three completely different factors: the ease of finding and following the path; the steepness or physical exertion; and of course, the length. All ten outings give clear directions on how to follow the trail, so they've been organized by what's left: the degree of effort and the length of trail.

Easy, Moderate or Strenuous

The book is organized with five pairings. These are *Easy and Short, Easy and Longer, Moderate and Short, Moderate and Longer,* and *Strenuous and Long.* This also gives you an easy reference for which hike to do next. If you'd like another of the same length and effort, try the trail in the same section. For a little tougher hike, step up to the following section; for a little easier one, drop down to the prior section.

Trail Descriptions

Each trail begins with a beautiful photo taken of or from the trail. This page also highlights *Hiking Time, Trail Length,* and *Elevation Change* (measured from lowest to highest points on the trail). This easy-to-read sidebar also features the nearest area in Red Rock Country that the trailhead is located *(Village of Oak Creek, West Sedona, Uptown Sedona,* or *Oak Creek Canyon).*

On the opposite page you'll find an introduction to the outing. This gives you a sense of what you'll experience.

Driving Directions come on the next page, with the aim of clearly guiding you to the right spot. The Sedona map (pages 4-5) is here as an additional driving reference.

Trail Notes highlight useful information, including restroom availability, weather and seasonal recommendations. It is smart to scan these before you begin.

The *Trail Description* offers in-depth narration so even the most inexperienced hikers will be able to follow the way. A colorful map provides highlights of the surroundings and for those that want them, GPS markings are there as a back-up for orientation. (See "GPS Data" on pages 108-110.)

With each trail you'll also find a general sidebar, offering insight on local history, wildlife or flora to add to the adventure.

Finally, *As Long As You're Here* offers suggestions for food or cultural spots nearby that can make a nice add-on to your hike.

Estimated Hiking Times

In general, the estimated hiking times will reflect expectations for a moderately healthy adult who has not walked the trail previously and is walking for enjoyment, rather than speed.

For your own reference, here are two more precise measurements. On terrain that is a little bit hilly, a relatively healthy adult walking at a normal pace and enjoying the views will average 1.5 miles per hour. That same person walking quickly over level ground without stopping will average 2.5 miles per hour.

PREPARING FOR YOUR SEDONA HIKE

Summer Hiking

Consider summer as lasting from May through September. In May and June, Sedona has hot sun and arid conditions. Summer heat lingers in the afternoon, as large areas of exposed sandstone radiate heat absorbed during the day.

In July and August the dryness is replaced by humidity, making these the least comfortable months of the year. This is the monsoon season, which features afternoon clouds, lightning, and sudden cloudbursts. The best strategy all summer long is to go out early, to take advantage of cool and dry conditions.

SEDONA WEATHER

Sedona's weather is renowned for its mildness. Sunshine splashes nearly year-round. Walking is a pleasure in every season, but understanding peculiarities of the high desert climate will help you avoid uncomfortable situations. Extreme conditions can arise.

Happy locals and awestruck visitors find Sedona's spring and autumn seasons about as good as it gets for being outdoors. Winds can be strong in the spring, so take caution on open areas and cliffsides such as Doe Mesa. In both seasons, temperatures plunge once the sun goes down, so places like Boynton Canyon and West Fork get cold fast. If you're planning on a sunset hike, bring warm clothing.

For an up-to-date weather forecast for Sedona visit:
www.sedonaweather.net.

Heat and Hydration

A remarkable number of walkers suffer from dehydration without even realizing it. Headache, fatigue and nausea are symptoms. It isn't that you won't recognize the heat. It's that you won't recognize the dryness, which sucks moisture out of your body at a devastating pace.

Drink one liter of water per hour (cool water, if possible) when hiking on hot summer days. Drink before you feel thirsty by taking a few sips of water every few minutes. This is more efficient for your body to absorb than gulping large quantities. Drink water especially when eating energy bars, trail mix, and other high-calorie foods. You'll dehydrate yourself further if you try to digest on a dry stomach.

Further, I'd consider investing in a hydration pack or a backpack with a hydration bladder. Yes, I know you've been told how much water to bring, but I'm going to tell you again. Bring plenty.

Winter Hiking

There's no need to rush out there in the winter as mornings begin cold. Plenty of sun and an average of just four snowfalls per year make this a great season to be outside. You should, however, beware of icy patches sometimes found on north-facing slopes and other places that remain shaded.

Clothing and Gear

Obviously, comfortable clothing and good walking shoes or boots are the smart gear choice. A hat with a broad brim will save your skin, as will a strong sunscreen. Day packs and fanny packs are best for holding extra items such as a personal first aid kit or gum to prevent cotton mouth.

I am a strong advocate of walking sticks, no matter your age. Consider them to be a 20-year extension on a warranty of good knees. They'll help you with balance, and reduce the jolt to your joints.

Altitude

At 4,500 feet above sea level, Sedona's altitude is not enough to make you sick, and there's no need for special acclimation. If you find yourself huffing and puffing, relax your pace, especially climbing hills.

Monthly Sunrise/Sunset and High/Low Temperatures
Sedona/Red Rock Country

Month		Sunrise	Sunset	High	Low
Jan	1	7:35 AM	5:27 PM	56°F	30°F
	15	7:35 AM	5:40 PM		
Feb	1	7:26 AM	5:56 PM	60°F	33°F
	15	7:13 AM	6:10 PM		
Mar	1	6:57 AM	6:23 PM	64°F	36°F
	15	6:38 AM	6:35 PM		
Apr	1	6:14 AM	6:48 PM	72°F	42°F
	15	5:56 AM	7:00 PM		
May	1	5:37 AM	7:13 PM	82°F	49°F
	15	5:24 AM	7:24 PM		
Jun	1	5:15 AM	7:36 PM	92°F	58°F
	15	5:13 AM	7:43 PM		
Jul	1	5:17 AM	7:45 PM	96°F	65°F
	15	5:25 AM	7:41 PM		
Aug	1	5:37 AM	7:30 PM	93°F	63°F
	15	5:48 AM	7:16 PM		
Sep	1	6:00 AM	6:54 PM	88°F	58°F
	15	6:10 AM	6:34 PM		
Oct	1	6:22 AM	6:11 PM	78°F	48°F
	15	6:33 AM	5:53 PM		
Nov	1	6:48 AM	5:33 PM	65°F	37°F
	15	7:01 AM	5:22 PM		
Dec	1	7:17 AM	5:16 PM	57°F	31°F
	15	7:28 AM	5:18 PM		

PRECAUTIONS

Wild Animals

Sedona's forests are home for a variety of interesting animals. From a hiker's point of view, there is little to fear, and lots to enjoy. The most likely times to see animals are in the early morning and early evening.

Mule deer, coyotes and javelinas may be sighted. There are no grizzly bears or wolves in the area and elk exist only in the high country. I'd be truly shocked if you saw a bobcat, mountain lion or black bear. However, they do exist deep in Sedona's wilderness. Give these wild animals space, and retreat slowly. They're not looking for a fight.

Snakes and Creepy Crawlers

On all the trails I've walked, I've seen only a half-dozen rattlesnakes, a few tarantulas and not a single scorpion. Sedona's cooler climate is less hospitable for these creatures than the deserts further south. The odds that you will see one are slim, so be cautious but not paranoid. Don't stick your hands into hidden places. Don't turn over rocks unnecessarily. If you are lucky enough to see one of these beautiful creatures, enjoy the moment but respectfully give it plenty of space.

Wildfire Season

Each summer, the Coconino National Forest is subject to potential closure to prevent forest fires. June and July are the most likely times for such extreme measures due to the dryness of the vegetation combined with the threat of lightning.

Yet at the same time, the Forest Service almost always leaves a few trails open. Check ahead rather than canceling your trip because of rumors. Call the Sedona Ranger Station at (928) 282-4119 for the most up-to-date information.

PHONE NUMBERS

NOTE: Don't take cellular phone service for granted: it is not widely reliable on Sedona's trails.

• CALL 911 to report a medical emergency, rescue situation, crime, or fire.

• SEDONA MEDICAL CENTER is Sedona's local hospital, located at 3700 W. Hwy 89A, nearly 4 miles west of the "Y" (89A/Hwy 179 intersection). 800-304-3004 or 928-204-3000 open 24 hours.

• SEDONA URGENT CARE provides medical assistance to walk-ins. 2530 W. Hwy 89A, 928-203-4813.

• LOCKSMITHS FOR LESS Locked the keys in the car? Call 928-282-5822.

ON YOUR WAY

Red Rock Pass

The walks and hikes covered in this book are located in the Coconino National Forest, and require a Red Rock Pass if you plan to park a car at the trailhead. These passes are widely available throughout town, not only at Forest Service Welcome Centers, but also at many retail stores. West Fork and Red Rock Crossing require special parking passes that can be purchased on site.

Trail Etiquette

Please, please, please stay on the main trails. Leaving them—also known as "bushwhacking"—is not only damaging to the land, it is unnecessary. In fact, it is arrogant: to visit and assume you're going to find a better route by going elsewhere doesn't make sense.

Allow folks walking uphill to have the right of way. Leave the wildflowers and cactus fruits alone for everyone to see. If you've got a dog, please keep it on a leash when around others and pick up after it does its business. Remove your own toilet paper (using a plastic bag) as a way to keep our forests clean of unsightly and unsanitary trash.

Most of all, make sure to let someone know where you will be hiking and sign in at the start of the trail.

MY WISH FOR YOUR VISIT

You should expect something special when you walk in Sedona. Treat nature with respect, and it will return more to you than can be logically explained. It will clear your mind for new ideas, uncover the vistas of fresh dreams and lighten any load your heart bears.

Nature has done all this and more for me. If you let Sedona in, it will change you too.

See you on the trails!

Village of Oak Creek

Hiking Time:
1 hour, 10 minutes
to Bell Rock and back.

2 hours, 5 minutes
for Courthouse Loop.

Trail Length:
2.2 miles
for Bell Rock rountrip.

4 miles
for Courthouse Loop.

Elevation Change:
250 feet up
to Bell Rock.

370 feet up
on the Courthouse Loop.

Bell Rock and Courthouse Loop

A great beginner hike around one of Sedona's most famous spots

IF YOU'RE LOOKING FOR A NICE, gentle way to ease yourself into the beauty of Red Rock Country, this is it. The Bell Rock Pathway was completed in 1999, widening an existing trail. Improved signage and a new parking lot at the trailhead make this the most notable entry to nature for those arriving in Sedona from the south. It isn't the first trail in Sedona, but it's more than likely the first one you'll notice.

I like this trail because it's a no-brainer. There is no anxiety about getting lost, and the exercise comes from walking the trail rather than from trying to find it. Including the main pathway but looping away from it, this trail is a confidence builder, smooth and straight for the first mile with curves later on. It is the kind of trail that will teach you to read red rock terrain, adjust to an elevated altitude and understand your own walking pace.

If you are as new to hiking as you are to Sedona, then this is a trail with fine views that will allow you to safely explore while you're getting some exercise.

Driving Directions Bell Rock Pathway is located in the Village of Oak Creek, on Sedona's south side. From Uptown or from West Sedona, head to the intersection of Highway 179 and 89A, locally called the "Y," then turn south onto Hwy 179 and follow it for 6.2 miles. You'll pass Bell Rock, but continue one more mile to the entry for Bell Rock Pathway Vista. There is ample parking here. Driving time from Uptown Sedona is 11 minutes, although the ride back will be longer if the weekend crowds are arriving. For a short walk to Bell Rock, park in the small lot on the left just before the formation as you head south on Hwy 179.

Trail Notes

- No restroom here, but there are restrooms in the Outlet Mall (past Taco Bell in the southeast corner) as well as at the nearby gas stations.
- Pleasant to walk anytime of year. In summer, the walk is best early in the morning.
- If you're photographing Bell Rock, note that the shadows fall onto it at least 45 minutes before the actual sunset.
- Yes, you can park close to Bell Rock and just scramble around there.
- A Red Rock Pass can be purchased at a machine at the parking lot. Cash and credit cards are accepted. Cost is $5 for a day, $15 for a one week pass.
- Official names: BELL ROCK PATHWAY #96 and COURTHOUSE BUTTE LOOP #135.

Bell Rock and Courthouse Loop Trail

Begin at the Bell Rock Pathway Vista parking lot. Ⓐ The ramada offers a few pointers on the area and has a decent map posted on the wall. The trail heads east at first, and it is wide and easy to follow. The first views come as the trail turns left, heading north. If Bell Rock were your home, this path would be the driveway. In the distance to the left you'll notice the Castle Rock pillar and the Transept behind it, while the impressive Courthouse Butte sits to the right.

You'll pass trail signs for horse riders and the "Big Park Loop," but there's no need to be concerned about these. There are rarely any of the former on this trail, and the latter connects neighbors to their neighborhoods without adding much scenery to your outing.

When I was a boy, I remember a place called "Safety Town" that we visited as schoolchildren. Directed by the local police, we got to practice as pedestrians, bike riders and car drivers (the latter in electrified go-carts). Signs and streetlights were built kid-size. That's

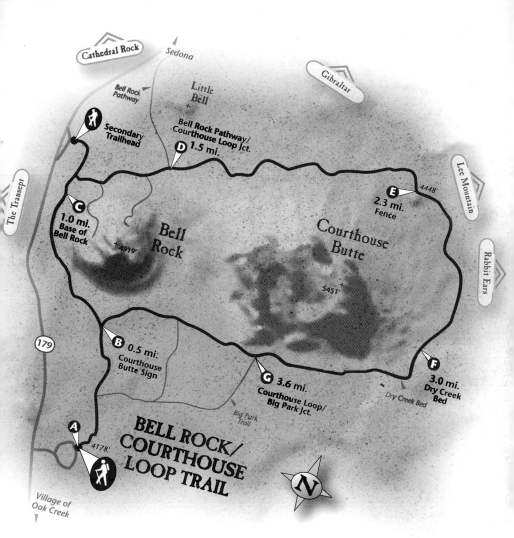

Cathedral Rock

Sedona

Gibraltar

Little Bell

Bell Rock Pathway

Bell Rock Pathway/ Courthouse Loop Jct.

D 1.5 mi.

Secondary Trailhead

The Transept

C 1.0 mi. Base of Bell Rock

Lee Mountain

4448'

E 2.3 mi. Fence

Rabbit Ears

Bell Rock

+4919'

Courthouse Butte

5451'+

179

B 0.5 mi. Courthouse Butte Sign

G 3.6 mi. Courthouse Loop/ Big Park Jct.

F 3.0 mi. Dry Creek Bed

Dry Creek Bed

Big Park Trail

A 4178'

BELL ROCK/ COURTHOUSE LOOP TRAIL

N

Village of Oak Creek

what I am reminded of each time I see the yellow signs cautioning "Curve Ahead." Are they placed there by a hyper-vigilant Forest Service...or does the Service just have a good sense of humor? After all, even if you are running, you won't be likely to be moving at more than a couple of miles an hour. The trail curve is so obvious at that slow speed that any warning is unnecessary.

Then I realized that not all who follow the path are walkers. Yes, bike riders may have their day here too. Is the sign telling them to watch out for slow walkers? Regardless, whether you walk or pedal, it is 1.1 miles to the far side of Bell Rock.

Halfway to Bell Rock (at 0.55 mile) is some signage worth noting. Ⓑ It points out the Courthouse Butte Loop to the right. I want you to take the loop, but for now continue straight ahead on the main pathway. Since this is a loop, you are basically just deciding whether to take it in a clockwise or counter-clockwise direction. I prefer the former, which saves the serenity behind the butte for later. The path has risen only 50 feet to this point, but the second half-mile to Bell Rock will gain 150 feet on a smooth incline.

You've been close to Bell Rock all along, but it isn't until you approach and round it from the left that you might feel like taking a run up onto it. Wait until you see the uphill path that is well-marked with wire baskets around red rock piles. Most of America marks its trails with "blazes." Such markings on trees work elsewhere, but here where there are large areas with no trees at all, an alternate indicator was required. Small rock piles known as *cairns* do the trick.

Cairns present two problems. Problem #1 is obvious: they're easily knocked down. Problem #2 is unexpected: they're easily built, often by folks who think they're doing the rest of us a favor by marking the trail. Only problem here is that they're often wrong. Instead of marking the correct trail, they've just marked the wrong one, usually a creek bed, dry wash or animal footpath. So rather than clearly signaling the correct trail, they've inadvertently paved the way for greater forest erosion.

The latest Forest Service solution is the cairn-on-steroids, a jumbo rock pile in mesh wiring that can't be knocked down and can't be ignored. So if you'd like to skip up the side of Bell Rock, follow these to any of the plateaus for a sit, a great view and possible mystical explorations.

I recommend going up part of the way, but not all of it. If you do, you'll add your name to a list of folks happy to make it up...and embarrassed to find they can't get down. Let Ropes That Rescue save somebody else today.

There's another path up Bell Rock just a few minutes ahead, also marked by a cairn on the right. This is another good reason to take the loop in a clockwise direction: you may decide to stay at Bell Rock and take the quickest way home after. In that case, turn around and return the way you came.

If you've got the energy to continue walking the loop, there's more good stuff ahead. First, nice views present themselves to the north as you walk east, crossing below Bell Rock. Ahead is Lee Mountain, with pointy Gibraltar Rock on its left side. Early-risers see the sun rising above this ridge; evening adventurers watch as the red rocks glow orange in color with the setting sun. Looking farther to the left you'll see the Twin Buttes, a pair of rocks with a saddle between them. At their lower left you can catch a glimpse of the Chapel of the Holy Cross. Postcards of the church taken up close show it dominating the rocks, but this long-distance perspective positions it humbly below the left-most of the buttes. This is the view those coming up Hwy 179—still a dirt road at the time the Chapel was built—would see as they rounded Bell Rock, perhaps seeing its cross lit up after sunset.

A flat open area presents you with a choice. The main Bell Rock Pathway heads left toward Little Bell, while the Courthouse Butte Loop heads off to your right. In high school my Latin teacher suggested that the round track had been invented for those of us on the track team who were too dumb to know when to stop. At least this way we couldn't head too far away. Regardless of what they taught you in high school, I recommend the loop. It is more removed from the highway and the crowds while offering great scenery. You'll also be

WHY ARE THE RED ROCKS RED?

Iron. Specifically, it is iron oxide, AKA rust. Iron shows up in stones such as feldspar. However, Sedona's iron is barely enough for measuring devices to notice. Instead, it seems to be distributed evenly and thinly.

Another color you'll notice is black. The long vertical marks on these rocks are made of manganese, AKA desert varnish, formed where water washes over the red rocks and reacts with iron oxide. It takes about a thousand years to form.

on a narrower trail and will have to pay a little bit closer attention to what's in front of you.

Do pause to look back every few minutes. After the Twin Buttes comes low, wide Airport Mesa as you turn your head left, with Capitol Butte behind it. This peak has been named and renamed at least five times. Some in town now call it Thunder Mountain, while others still know it as Grayback. Further west comes the fingered formation we call the Cockscomb. Again scanning to the left, before your eyes strike Cathedral Rock you'll see an open gap that looks different here—less photogenic— than it does when seen from the south. However, the gap is where to look if you're up really early: there may be hot air balloons floating there.

Although you can't cut between Bell and Courthouse, you'll still see plenty of both formations from the loop. More importantly, their shape and appearance will continue to change before your eyes. Even what you call them will change when you realize that they aren't truly mountains, but the edge of the Colorado Plateau. Formations like the ones you are circling did not rise up like the Rockies, but rather were part of the uplifted land that was not worn away by water and wind. Courthouse Butte is imposing, and rounding it feels like "the real thing," as if you've found a secret back door into Red Rock Country.

The trail zigs up and zags down, winding around the butte. From here you'll be following the wire-mesh cairns again. As you pass

With all the colors of the stones and trees, you may be surprised that Sedona's brightest tones come each spring during wildflower season. April and early May constitute peak season. Nonetheless, the first flowers are out in early March, and if you count the blossoms of yuccas and cacti, colorflul flowers last throughout the summer and even into autumn in Sedona.

Since no two years bring identical weather, flowers take turns arriving. Therefore, it is difficult to say exactly what you'll see, and where and when you'll see it. At some point, you're certain to see a few of the following most common flowers. *Verbenas* are small, purple and nice-smelling. *Penstemons* are most prevalent in their bright red version, while *cliff roses* blossom on a shrub. While blooms don't last long, the aroma is fantastically sweet. *Asters* come in white and purple, as do *fleabanes*. *Indian paintbrush* is orange-red in color, but not as big as *desert primroses* which are white, low to the ground and close up at night. *Owl clover* flourishes in open grasslands (see photo).

through a fenced area, note that you've walked more than two and a quarter miles. Ⓒ A small but tempting hillock is off to your left as you follow the narrowing trail back south and then east, above a creek bed. I call it "Cheesecake," but you're free to give it your own name. Visible to the east (looking away from the butte) is the tall, split pillar whose name, Rabbit Ears, is well-known.

The views of Courthouse Butte continue to evolve. The formation seems to be growing taller, in part because your elevation begins to drop. You may spy a dry creek bed to your left, and eventually the trail will take you across it. I'd begin to peek around here for pools and puddles of water, which make for good photo opportunities. Following now along the left side of the creek bed, continue past the cairns until you are unmistakably led back into the dry wash.

On one occasion I was walking here when one of Sedona's spring snow storms hit late in April. Even when you know it's coming, it is a surprise to see it, in part because it is often a sunny 72 degrees the day before and the day after. Anyway, that evening walk brought big wet flakes that quickly melted and drained through here, creating gentle flows and soothing sounds in the wash.

This being Sedona, chances are that you're more likely to see sun than snow. The only white stuff will be the flowers of the banana yucca, providing a nice photograph against the red rock background. The terrain here is classic Piñon-Juniper Forest, or what locals like to call High Desert. Prickly pear cacti, strawberry hedgehog cacti (see photo) and manzanita bushes with mahogany-colored bark rest at your feet, with small mourning doves and Gambel's quail foraging among them.

At the wash are signs leading in two directions. Ⓓ To the left is the Big Park Loop, and to the right is Courthouse Butte Loop. I consider

the former more of a connector trail for locals to their homes. The views are prettier to the right, and you'll soon see the butte's most impressive face.

Over the next few minutes, you'll walk a bit closer to the butte. I'd like to direct your attention to the beauty and diversity of its red face. There are chunky, putty-style forms; thin strata-like layers; and checkerboard patterns. Look more closely and you'll notice several vertical gray and black stripes. Water flows down here during rain showers. Imagine the wonder of waterfalls on Courthouse Butte.

What you shouldn't be directing your attention toward are the numerous "social" trails that appear mostly to your right. These are unofficial paths, and they will lead you astray. Notice also that as the butte has grown more impressive, Bell Rock appears to look smaller, as if its top had been chopped off.

In just under four miles, you close the loop with the Bell Rock Pathway. The return walk to the pathway is a distance of a little more than half a mile. (E) This is one trail in Sedona where you are certain to find people just beginning as you come to an end. I always think, "What should I tell them? What good advice should I give?" In the end, I just smile, and wish them a good outing.

Likewise, I think you'll enjoy your outing. You can always return to the pathway, but I hope it will give you the confidence to try some new trails among the red rocks.

As Long as You're Here There are several gas stations within 1 mile of the parking lot for drinks and supplies. If you'd rather bike the trail than walk it, check out Sedona Bike & Bean. It is across the road from the parking lot, a little closer to the stoplight. For souvenirs and art, stop in at Sedona Trading Post, one block south.

Less than a mile south on Hwy 179, the Outlet Mall offers shopping. The Marketplace Café is here, for an excellent lunch. South through the next stoplight is the Tequa Plaza. Enjoy wine-tasting at A'Roma or The Art of Wine, or a delicious dinner at romantic Cucina Rustica.

West Sedona

Hiking Time:
30 to 40 minutes
for a roundtrip.

Trail Length:
Up to **1.5 miles**
for the entire roundtrip.

Elevation Change:
60 to 70 feet up.
The trailhead parking
area is 4,050 feet.

Cathedral Rock
at Red Rock Crossing

This walk offers you views
rather than taking you onto
Cathedral Rock itself.

CONSIDERED THE MOST PHOTOGRAPHED
image in Arizona after the Grand Canyon,
Cathedral Rock speaks to both power and
gentleness. On the one hand, it seems a natural
fortress, with a river and red rocks replacing moat
and drawbridge, like something you would make if
you were good enough with sand castles. Yet with
its grouped formations and wonderful colors—red
is just one of many you'll see here—it also seems
somehow approachable, hardly intimidating.

The walk itself offers you the best views of
Cathedral rather than taking you onto the mountain
itself. You may choose between the ultra-gentle path
on the park side or an easy trail across the creek.
Either way, your gaze will shift from the nearby water
to the far-off formation over and over again. That's
just fine: with a distance of under a mile each way,
there's no rush.

Driving Directions From West Sedona, head west on 89A in the direction of Cottonwood. The last stoplight in town is 4.1 miles from the "Y" at Upper Red Rock Loop Road. Turn left at the light and continue on past Red Rock High School on the right. Pay attention to the sharp curves and turn left 1.8 miles ahead. This is Chavez Ranch Road. A small sign on the right is easy to miss, but it points out Crescent Moon Ranch and Red Rock Crossing. To be clear, Crescent Moon Ranch is the name of the park; Red Rock Crossing is the scenic point on Oak Creek where vehicles once crossed. Now stay on this road through its sharp banking right-hand curve just short of its end, about a half-mile up. On the left is the park entrance, through which you must go to reach Red Rock Crossing.

Trail Notes

- Environmental toilets are in the parking lot at Crescent Moon Ranch.
- Anytime of year is a good time for this trail.
- In warmer months, check with the park attendants to ensure that the creek water is safe for swimming.
- Late afternoon beats the early morning for the best photos of Cathedral Rock.
- Parking fees and times vary with the season. Usually it costs $8 to enter and the hours are 9am-8pm.
- Note that Cathedral Rock has several trails and approaches. The entrance via Back O' Beyond off Hwy 179 leads to a strenuous uphill trail with great views.
- Official name: TEMPLETON TRAIL #156 and BALDWIN TRAIL #191.

Cathedral Rock at Red Rock Crossing
Trail on north side of creek

For the gentle route, simply follow the sidewalk for a path that stays close to Oak Creek. The sidewalk leads from the Crescent Moon Ranch parking lot to the creek, where you can walk over to the benches and have a sit, or turn left to follow the sidewalk through the park toward the old mill wheel. The sidewalk continues for half a mile, then turns to a dirt trail as you pass the mill. In the woods here, there are several opportunities to get closer to the water. The first comes almost immediately. Stepping off the trail over some branches you can reach the creek to see "The Falls." It's not Niagara, but it sure is a pretty setting for a little waterfall. It draws children to swim in the summer.

Back on the main trail, your second opportunity comes two minutes ahead, where a gentle finger of the stream winds through the cottonwoods. It's another nice spot to stop.

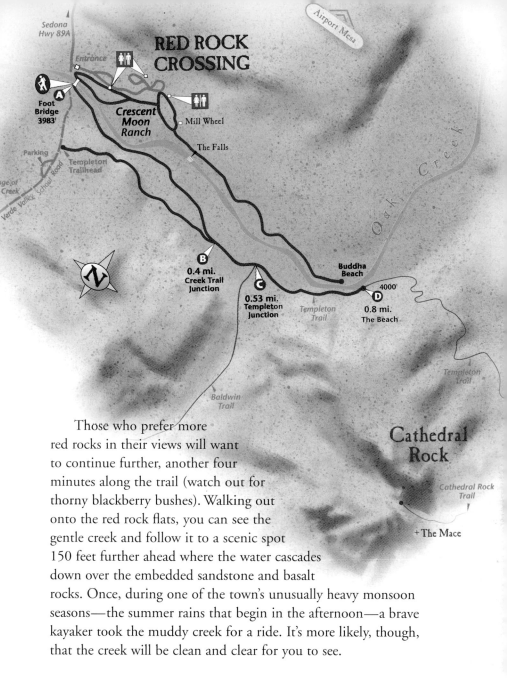

RED ROCK CROSSING

Sedona Hwy 89A

Airport Mesa

Entrance

Foot Bridge 3983'

Parking

Templeton Trailhead

Village of Oak Creek

Verde Valley School Road

Crescent Moon Ranch

Mill Wheel

The Falls

Oak Creek

A

N

B 0.4 mi. Creek Trail Junction

C 0.53 mi. Templeton Junction

Templeton Trail

Buddha Beach

D 4000'

0.8 mi. The Beach

Baldwin Trail

Templeton Trail

Cathedral Rock

Cathedral Rock Trail

+The Mace

Those who prefer more red rocks in their views will want to continue further, another four minutes along the trail (watch out for thorny blackberry bushes). Walking out onto the red rock flats, you can see the gentle creek and follow it to a scenic spot 150 feet further ahead where the water cascades down over the embedded sandstone and basalt rocks. Once, during one of the town's unusually heavy monsoon seasons—the summer rains that begin in the afternoon—a brave kayaker took the muddy creek for a ride. It's more likely, though, that the creek will be clean and clear for you to see.

Trail on south side of creek

For something a little less crowded, try the path across the creek to get closer to Cathedral Rock. From the park, follow the sidewalk to the right (as you face the creek, i.e., south) to head toward the wooden

Optional Driving Directions From the Village of Oak Creek take Hwy 179 to the stoplight at Verde Valley School Road just south of the outlet mall. Driving from the "Y," this intersection is 7.1 miles. Turn right onto Verde Valley School Road and go 4.6 miles (paved for a while, then changes to a groomed dirt road) to the parking lot on the left.

Rather than taking the trailhead here, walk 150 yards down the road to the creek. From this side you can reach Red Rock Crossing without entering Crescent Moon Ranch. You'll avoid the park's fee, but currently need a Red Rock Pass to use the parking lot, although they aren't sold here.

plank that serves as a footbridge. Ⓐ Once you've crossed over the tiny bridge, turn left and follow along the red rocks, walking in the direction of Cathedral Rock. If you've driven in via the unpaved Verde Valley School Road, walk 150 yards beyond the parking lot to the creek. To join this path turn right at the end of the road. Ⓑ Home to sunbathers and meditators, this pleasant area is a nice place to stop and sit by the water. A feeling of serenity is almost unavoidable here. Some enterprising local ministers utilize the spot for weddings, and they've got it down pat, from string quartets to doves—all the elements for the perfect outdoor wedding here in one place.

If you headed no further you could call your entire Sedona experience a success. Walking will bring rewards though, especially if you continue on the red rock flats until they seem to end. Two minutes ahead, walking along the red rock flats toward Cathedral Rock, the trail divides. Choose the low, narrow, center path that leads into the leafy forest.

As you follow this route, do your best to keep quiet. First, it will help you to experience the riparian life zone you've entered. Second, you might just see the turtle who sits on the fallen tree branch in the marsh pool on the left. Too much noise and all you'll hear is the "plop" after she drops in the water to escape your view. It's a lovely walk through here, but it sure doesn't feel like Arizona. The stony path leads you up along more red rocks on a narrow trail that squeezes by a tree and skirts blackberry bushes.

Three minutes ahead, you'll notice the trail becomes sandy. There is a side trail to the left here that crosses another creek finger (usually dry, except in mid-spring) and heads to the main creek. Alternatively, you may continue through the sand as the trail brings you to Cathedral Rock less than 10 minutes ahead. Emerging through the trees, the formation impresses anyone who sees it from this vantage point. Ⓒ There is no stream before it, just red rock pillars in four parts. The center-right formation is called Lover's Rock, and you might make out the man and woman standing back-to-back. Personally, I've always seen it as a hand forming a peace sign, with the two fingers together and the thumb down to the left. I call it "The Invisible Hand," because when you look back from Highway 179 (which you may perhaps take to leave town), the formation seems to have disappeared. Exactly in its spot is an open gap. Hmm.

You can continue through this meadow, which seems to flaunt new colors every week through spring into early summer. Purple owl clover and white-colored desert primrose emerge in April, giving way to the flowering yuccas and grasses, with brown-purple seeds atop.

WHAT IS A VORTEX?

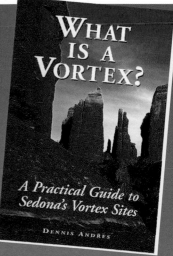

Each year, thousands of visitors to Sedona have something extraordinary happen to them. Whether it shows up as inexplicable tears or a tingling in the hands, the source seems to be Sedona's mystical energy vortices. Yet after decades of reported phenomena, a clear explanation remains elusive.

The most widely-mentioned theory—that the iron in the red rocks is creating a magnetic field—has little evidence to support it. On the other hand, that Sedona has impacted thousands of people over a number of years cannot be denied.

More likely, what people are feeling is not magnetism but "subtle energy." The realm of alternative healers, this is something not perceptible to your standard five senses. Yet it is very real, and those with a stronger sensitivity to intuition, energy and emotion are able to feel it. There is increasing evidence that places of natural beauty and sacred sites around the world are areas where subtle energy is strongest. Given that subtle energy isn't strictly physical, there's no need to find the right "spot" to stand on.

Instead, find a place that you feel drawn to, sit and close your eyes, then let yourself enjoy the good feelings. To visit some of the famous vortex areas in Sedona try the hikes to Bell Rock, Cathedral Rock at Red Rock Crossing, Boynton Canyon, and Munds Wagon Trail on Schnebly Hill.

For a more descriptive explanation, consult one of my other books: *What Is A Vortex? A Practical Guide to Sedona's Vortex Sites.*

At the fork in the trail, you'll find before your eyes a picture that ought to be inserted in the dictionary next to the word "tree." Ⓓ It's a perfectly formed Arizona cypress.

The right fork up ahead of you is pleasant but leads nowhere in particular along the Baldwin Trail. If you want to go on, take the left fork, which brings you closer to the creek via the Templeton Trail. The trail features a long rope from a branch overhanging the creek, which becomes a source of much fun in the summer. Half a mile up, the trail will bank left by a small beach, and you'll see across to Sedona's outdoor art gallery for budding rock-pile makers. Anybody can make a cairn, but it takes an real artist to balance the biggest rocks on top here at Buddha Beach.

If you're on the art-enhanced side of the creek, you've come to the end of the trail. This makes a good turnaround point, too, for those on the south side of the creek, although the trail does continue through a nice forest before climbing severely to reach the north side of Cathedral Rock.

Before you return, spend a couple of minutes by the stream. Here, as it washes over the creek stones and makes a sharp turn, it creates lovely sounds. You might notice that you feel a bit different than when you arrived. More relaxed, more calm, breathing easily and feeling generally "lighter," you may realize that it takes little effort to invite Sedona's gentle magic. It all happens naturally.

As Long as You're Here If coming via West Sedona, check out Canyon Outfitters at 2701 W. Hwy 89A for gear and supplies. The approach from this side to Crescent Moon Ranch is extremely scenic. Upper Red Rock Loop Road offers a number of undeveloped pullouts on the left-hand side as you drive down the hill. If you bypass the turn onto Chavez Ranch Road, the road turns to gravel and dirt, eventually arriving at lovely Red Rock State Park. Although not as beautiful as Red Rock Crossing, this state park has a nice visitor center and gentle trails.

Oak Creek Canyon

Hiking Time:
3 hours, 30 minutes
for the complete hike.

Trail Length:
Up to **6.4 miles**
for the entire roundtrip.

It is 3.2 miles each way.

Elevation Change:
250 feet up, although
the grade is hardly
noticeable. The start of
the trail is 5,260 feet.

West Fork

**Awesome cliffs mingle beside
a gentle stream to create a
sense of pure magic.**

THE CANYON ZANE GREY LOVED
enough to memorialize in 1924, in his
The Call of the Canyon novel, has been enjoyed
by presidents, royalty, and hikers ever since. Here
awesome cliffs mingle beside a gentle stream to
create a sense of pure magic. Walk it and you may
find yourself falling in love with nature.

If you crave red rocks and solitude, the lush
greenery and weekend crowds should keep this from
being your only Sedona hike. Even so, know that
things will be easy here. There's beauty around
every corner of this three-and-a-half-hour adventure,
with little effort required. A recent flood has altered
crossings of the creek, but not the beauty.

Walk West Fork with someone who matters to
you. Invite someone with whom you are, or would
like to be, in love. It is Sedona's most romantic trail.
Plan a picnic and stay for a while, knowing that
in West Fork the experience is more important than
the exercise.

Driving Directions From the "Y," head north on Hwy 89A through Uptown Sedona, over Midgely Bridge and through the lovely Oak Creek Canyon. After you pass Don Hoel's Cabins on the right, you've got less than a mile to go. You're there when you see a sign for parking, and immediately after it you'll turn left into the parking lot and stop at the small check-in station. The parking fee is $8 and is not covered by the Red Rock Pass. Driving time from Uptown Sedona is 25 minutes; from the Village of Oak Creek it is 35 minutes.

Trail Notes

- Environmental toilets in the parking area.
- All 15 or so creek crossings are easy and none require wading. The only real uphill comes in the final 10 minutes.
- Expect temperatures 8 degrees cooler than in Uptown Sedona.
- Crowded on summer and autumn weekends, especially later in the day.
- Wear sandals to splash through the cool water and beat summer heat.
- Be alert for minor patches of poison ivy.
- This is Sedona's best trail for autumn foliage, seen in October and November.
- I don't recommend West Fork for the winter. Although beautiful, it is cold and icy.
- Official name: WEST FORK, #108.

West Fork Trail

Leaving the parking lot, pass the "Call of the Canyon" signboard and walk along the path. Ⓐ It leads you to a new bridge above the stream. There are areas of interest here, although you haven't yet come to the true trailhead. A quarter-mile ahead, passing through orchards that date back to the first settlers, sign your name into the registration book and turn right to follow the trail, #108. Ⓑ The first spot of interest is the old ruins that were once home to Bear Howard, one of Sedona's legendary settlers (see "Sedona's Favorite Bear" sidebar, pg. 102). Years later they were improved to form the Mayhew Lodge. It was famous for its hospitality, serving as a getaway for movie stars and diplomats. This is where the true trail begins.

The trail is relatively well marked. You may find it dividing into two separate trails in many spots, but these are simply alternate routes along which to follow the creek. In most cases, they will still get you to the same place. In 2002, substantial work was done to enhance the main trail. Now plenty of cairns mark the path, especially at creek crossings.

The good stuff begins almost immediately. Just a minute past the trail map and signage, you'll sense the still water and the high-rising cliffs to your left. The pools will reflect the hanging ferns and flowers that take advantage of water running down the sides of the cliffs. Take a photo if you like, but know that there is much more to come.

The creek crossing is the first of approximately 15 between here and the end of the day trail. Ⓒ So let's review a few pointers. First, test logs and stones to determine how stable they are. Second, don't walk on a log by itself. Rather, use it to straddle the water with another log or with stones. Stick to dry stones if possible. Finally, if all else fails, don't be afraid to simply walk in the water. It isn't deep, and the streambed may be sturdier for you than the stones across it.

Boulder
2.2 mi.
Ⓔ

Flagstaff

West Fork

89A

Oak Creek

6748'

Ⓓ
1.2 mi.
5th
Crossing

Parking
Ⓐ
5330'

Trail Kiosk
0.3 mi.
Ⓑ

N

Mayhew's
Lodge Ruins

Ⓒ
0.8 mi.
1st Crossing

WEST FORK
TRAIL

6700'

Sedona

From Westerns to sport utility vehicle commercials, Sedona and film have long gone together. The connection began right here at West Fork. Zane Grey was an Ohioan who fell in love with the West. He trekked across it, hunted in it, and most of all, wrote about it. *Riders of The Purple Sage* was not only a hit as a book in 1912, but soon became a movie.

Not long after Grey wrote *The Call of the Canyon*, Paramount Studios made a motionpicture of it, the first of dozens of films to be made in the area. Other directors and stars followed, from John Wayne to Joan Crawford, Jimmy Stewart (who made *Broken Arrow*) to Henry Fonda, Elvis Presley to Robert DeNiro.

Today, Sedona boasts its own "studio," the Zaki Gordon Institute for Independent Film-making, as well as the Sedona International Film Festival, held each March. Keep this in mind when you think that Sedona is a place that ought to be in pictures: it is!

Again, the crossing is so nice that it wouldn't be a crime to stop and explore right here. The area to the right of the first crossing is also beautiful, with cave walls hanging low over placid water. All things considered, however, I say it is better to keep moving. Get as far along this beautiful canyon as you are willing, and then pick your spot. Reward those feet of yours and dip them in the shallow water. Let yourself feel like a kid again.

Remember to look up every now and then. Two minutes past the first crossing a face appears high in the white sandstone above. Polling data suggests respondents are divided on whether it is a Native American elder, a mummy or a fish. I've decided to call it "Chief Mummy Fish-Face." No disrespect intended.

A mile and 40 minutes in, you'll come to the fifth creek crossing, my favorite. Ⓓ Stepping around a tall tree to some angular embedded rocks, you'll drop from right to left down to the stream. Here the narrowed creek widens as it slides down a slanted slab. Over the slab the water forms a pool, and you can see freshwater trout swimming upstream. Although I label it as a creek crossing, the truth is that the better trail is now on the same side of the creek.

Like mermaids calling sailors to the ocean depths, West Fork seduces you to walk into its canyons. Curiously, there is so much beauty in general that no one spot in particular stands out. Instead, note the colors that stand out. In spring and summer lush greens are polka-dotted by the purple of lupine flowers, and striped by the orange bark of ponderosa pine trees.

West Fork serves as Sedona's best getaway for beating the summer heat, but autumn will always be its most famous season. Zane Grey's hero said it best in *The Call of the Canyon:*

> Here in the canyon you'd think there was blazing fire everywhere.
> The vines and maples are red, scarlet, carmine, cerise, magenta,
> all the hues of flame. The oak leaves are turning russet gold, and
> the sycamores are yellow green.

The book became Sedona's first Western, the first of many Hollywood films made in Red Rock Country. Jimmy Stewart, Henry Fonda, Joan Crawford, Robert Mitchum, John Wayne and yes, even Elvis made Westerns here.

Other points to watch for include the massive rectangular boulder in the stream, resting as if it had been airlifted in and placed there. (Look for the connect-the-dots paint around the lichen.) A half-mile farther there is an arch-like shape in the red rock cliff side. Then there's another boulder on the left side of the trail, and the landslide that brought it down is to your right.

There's an excellent spot about 2.7 miles along the trail, but you may not notice it until you turn around and return. As the trail cruises along, rising higher with the creek at your lower left, you'll notice a nice patch of flat red rock. It looks great for sitting upon, and so it is: you can even swing your feet out over the edge. However, if you walk two minutes further you'll find a route down to the creek. Coming back, you'll see the ridge extends long enough to earn the name "The Subway." Sitting underneath it, you can picnic while listening secretly to hikers passing up above.

After that, the trail becomes a bit of a mess. There have been several tree-falls and probably some floods that have made the trail a bit more difficult to follow. If there's a choice between a big pyramid-style cairn and a small one, pick the big one. However, in most cases now there are fewer official markings.

As you enter the final portion of the trail, you'll climb the only uphill stretch of the hike. It is a rise of 75 feet, bringing you high above the creek, which will be on your right. As you drop down again, realize that all the creek crossings up to this point could be accomplished (at least in principle) without getting your feet very wet. I expect the 15th creek crossing will be the one you'll neither ford, nor forget.

Here the creek is attractively wedged between two sinuous walls curving to the right. Unless you are an ambitious explorer looking for deeper canyon adventures, the chilly water is your sign that it is time to turn around.

The Return Route

If you've rushed through West Fork too quickly, relax: you're going to get a second chance to see it. Once your anxiety of wondering "Will we get to the end?" has been erased, you'll know how far you have to go and about how long it will take. So enjoy it.

Again, keep your eyes open for "The Subway." This overhang of rock will be noticeable after 20 minutes of walking back from the very end of the day trail.

As you come to the home stretch, take another look across the creek up at the towering walls. It is a chance to memorize how majestic West Fork is. On your way through the orchards, you can envy the owners of those nice homes across the creek, and seek out blackberry bushes by the foot bridge.

As Long as You're Here One of the nicest benefits of hiking West Fork is the drive from Sedona to get there. Traveling north on 89A through Oak Creek Canyon, you pass through the most historic parts of Sedona. This is one trail where the beauty begins on the drive, which will lead you 10 miles north. You can stop at the Oak Creek Canyon Visitor Center for information, historic Garland's for Native American jewelry, or Indian Gardens for sandwiches on fresh-baked bread. The café at Junipine Resort offers outdoor seating, beer, wine, and a variety of fine dishes including trout.

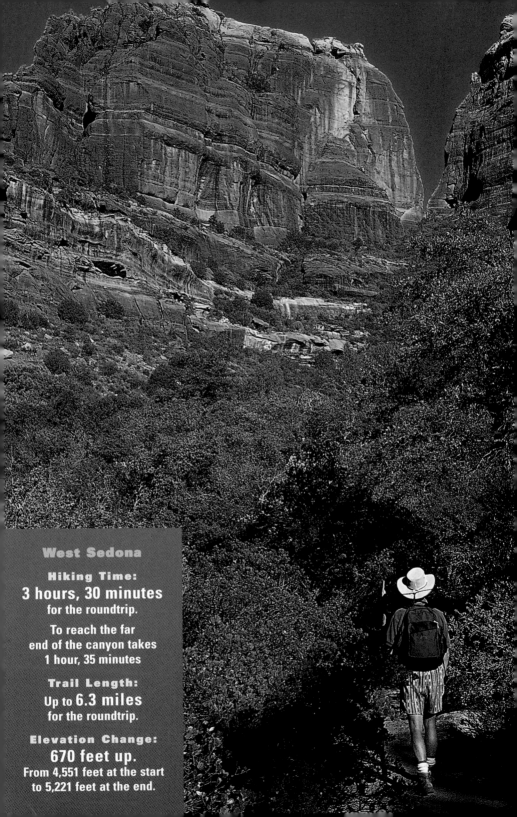

West Sedona

Hiking Time:
3 hours, 30 minutes
for the roundtrip.

To reach the far
end of the canyon takes
1 hour, 35 minutes

Trail Length:
Up to **6.3 miles**
for the roundtrip.

Elevation Change:
670 feet up.
From 4,551 feet at the start
to 5,221 feet at the end.

Boynton Canyon

Touch the sacred in this deep red canyon

C AN A PLACE BE TOO BEAUTIFUL for its own good? From its open canyon spaces and towering cliff walls to sheltered spots amid shady pine trees, Boynton Canyon is stunning and varied. The special areas here create a good mood in just about everyone who enters them. If you're hearty enough to walk it end-to-end, you'll agree with a hiker I passed recently who said, "It's a little bit of heaven."

At the same time, Boynton Canyon has its drawbacks. First, the trail has become popular and crowded. Second, the path is neither short, nor perfectly flat, in contradiction to the expectations of uninformed tourists. Third, for 25 minutes the trail parallels a resort, which although lovely, interrupts wilderness with civilization.

There is good news. The 2004 opening of a new trailhead and parking lot is helping to ease the congestion. Solitude is still possible—just avoid spring and autumn weekends, or come early if you can't. Then watch as your spirit is lifted in the sheltering glory of Boynton Canyon!

Driving Directions From the "Y," head west on Hwy 89A for three miles to the stoplight at Dry Creek Road. Turn right and follow Dry Creek Road for 2.8 miles to the stop sign, then turn left onto FR 152C, also called Boynton Pass Road. Follow this road for 1.5 miles to a stop sign. Go right for 0.1 mile to the parking lot on the right. Be aware that it may be crowded. The new lot has 27 parking spots, which is still too few but a lot more than the old one had. Driving time is under 20 minutes from the center of town; 30 minutes from the Village of Oak Creek.

Trail Notes

- Environmental toilets in the parking area, but no access to the resort restrooms.
- Note that the interior canyon is much cooler than the warm, exposed trailhead.
- Beat the crowd: come early!
- Watch for monsoons in July and August, which can lead to minor flooding (up to your ankles) in canyon drainages.
- Sorry, there's no sunset here. However, the east canyon walls are pretty in afternoon light.
- Staying at Enchantment? Lucky you! Access the trail via the resort's back gate with your room card (0.3 mi. from the lobby), or via an access gate behind the spa.
- Official Name: BOYNTON CANYON, #47.

Boynton Canyon Trail

Once upon a time the only place to get lost in Boynton Canyon was at the start, but a new trailhead completed in 2004 has put an end to that. Trail access is a tricky decision for the Forest Service. On the one hand, nobody likes to find that there is no parking. On the other hand, limited parking tends to limit access to the trails, keeping down the numbers and the damage. Ⓐ

The trail kiosk is close to the road. Sign in and follow the trail downward until it forks a few minutes ahead. Turn left at the sign, and follow the trail past the remains of the old parking lot. You'll get a clearer view of the spire up to your right, which appears to have a stone plopped on top. A trail sign lists Boynton Spire and advises hikers that access to the resort is for guests only. This spire is also known to locals as Kachina Woman.

While you're passing alongside the resort and nearby residences, I'll tell you a little about the canyon. Boynton Canyon plays a significant role in the creation story of the Yavapai Indians, who continue to live in the Verde Valley today. The canyon was named for a pioneer who sheltered stock here, though his name is spelled differently.

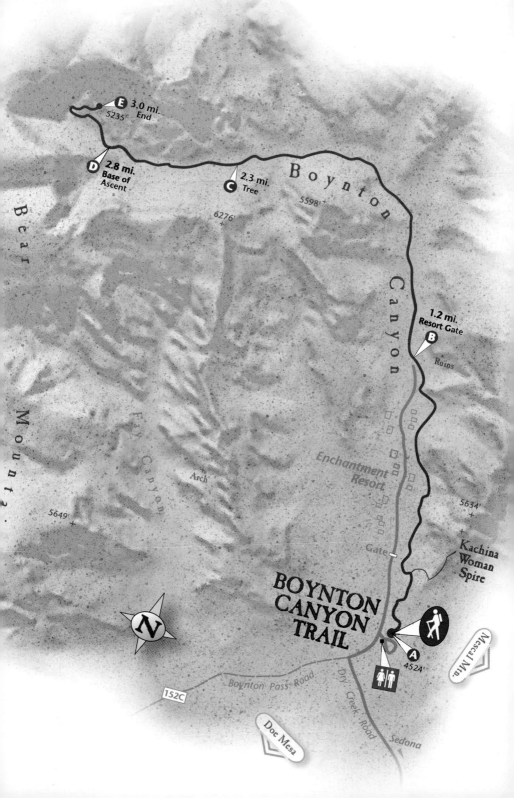

E 3.0 mi. End
5235'

D 2.8 mi. Base of Ascent

C 2.3 mi. Tree

Boynton Canyon

5598'

6276'

1.2 mi. Resort Gate **B**

Ruins

Bear Mountain

Fay Canyon

Arch

Enchantment Resort

5634'

5649'

Gate

Kachina Woman Spire

BOYNTON CANYON TRAIL

Mescal Mtn.

4524' **A**

N

Boynton Pass Road

152C

Dry Creek Road

Doc Mesa

Sedona

Today, the canyon is home to luxurious Enchantment Resort. Amenities include a conference center, a restaurant and grill, tennis courts, and several swimming pools. The newest item at the resort is what you're about to walk past: Mii Amo, a spa, opened in early 2001. As you walk, you can fantasize about staying there someday.

Further along, you'll pass by and scan some private homes in the canyon, including that of Y.A. Title, former N.Y. Giants football great. Sadly, your only interaction with these residents is the nasty warning sign threatening video surveillance and armed patrols. Let me make a few points here. First, I have personally met hikers who misinterpreted the sign as meaning that they had to turn around here. It does not. Second, as someone who has spent plenty of time inside the resort,

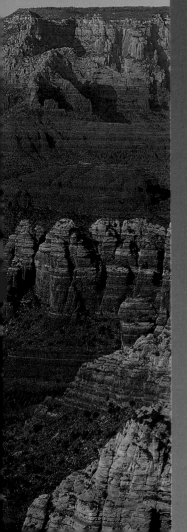

SEDONA GEOLOGY 101

To understand our geology think of it as a three-part play.

I. Water. Much of what you're seeing today was once under water. About 350 million years ago, ocean covered this area. It receded, but this was just the first of several eras when water would overflow this land, laying down layers of sand, or eroding away land that was here. For that reason, almost all the rock you can see in Sedona is sandstone. Great for hiking on, but bad news for climbers who find the rock too soft to support them.

II. Land. Although the hills around you may appear to be mountains, they are in fact the edge of the Colorado Plateau. 65 million years ago two tectonic plates (Pacific and North American) slid alongside each other. When the heavier plate slipped underneath the other, it uplifted the lighter plate to create the massive Colorado Plateau, which extends into southern Utah, western New Mexico and southwestern Colorado.

III. Volcanoes. Few people realize that there are more than 800 volcanoes on the Plateau. Several million years ago lava flowed through some parts of Sedona. On some of Sedona's highest ridges, such as Wilson Mountain, you can notice a chocolate-gray layer. It's basalt, the lava rock laid down several million years ago. Tougher and rougher than sandstone, it will last a lot longer than Sedona's red and blond cliffs.

See page 111 for more geology information including an illustrated chart of Sedona's geologic strata.

that might be a camera, but I don't think anybody is taping. Third, the only "armed patrol" here are the javelina. The truth is the homeowners deserve their privacy...and the hikers deserve not to be insulted.

The first mile of the trail ends as you pass the resort's back gate, and here the real beauty begins. Ⓑ About 40 paces past the small entry trail, you can begin looking over your right shoulder to the corner canyon. Where the red rock rises above the green trees, a shady alcove hosts ancient ruins of the Sinagua civilization.

The trail will turn back to the right (north) as you enter one the most beautiful parts of the canyon. Here, where the gap between the east and west walls of the canyon narrows, you'll feel the canyon so close that it seems to caress you. Ahead lies the "Boynton Bowling Alley," a straight, sandy chute offering new views of higher blond sandstone ridges in the distance. The alley is three-fifths of a mile long, after which you'll notice taller pines and you'll take a pair of left-hand turns. These turns bring you from open-air views into the deeper canyon. Off to the right side, you may notice the dry wash down below you.

If you've come this far, Boynton rewards you with an entirely new terrain. Suddenly you're in the forest, with Arizona cypress and ponderosa pine trees that look big enough to hug. Passing the two-mile mark, I encourage you to get close to the orange-tinted bark of a tall ponderosa. Stick your nose in and take a sniff. Most folks smell vanilla, but it always seems more like praline pecan to me. Mmm! Ahead you'll see the stump of a fallen grandfather pine on the left side of the trail. I miss its majesty, but it still marks the way. Ⓒ

Lots of people love Boynton Canyon, but what is even more magical is that this is one canyon that will love you back. Just stop for a moment. Pause to breathe in the air and feel the joy and pleasure of knowing that you are here. Whether you traveled thousands of miles or just a few, whether you came to reconnect with a past life or to dream up a new future, your being here is no accident.

After an hour or more of walking, you'll enter the third and final mile of the trail. While the first mile is open and wide, the second feels tall and narrow. To me, the third mile feels uphill, as half of the canyon's 670 feet of vertical gain will come at this point.

On every occasion in Boynton Canyon I've encountered people who begin to ask "How much farther?" and "Is it worth it?" These questions are usually asked by folks who are starting to tire out.

Boynton is only described as an easy trail by folks who don't go all the way to the end! Boynton is easy to follow, yes, but the final mile will make anybody's heart beat faster. Remember, the question isn't "Can I make it to the end?" but "Can I make it to the end and back?"

If you do choose to push on, here are your rewards: First, the leafy canyon will close in on you with bigtooth maple, oaks and other lush trees. You'll notice how cool it is back here, as compared with the exposed start of the trail. Second, you'll criss-cross a dry creek bed, making you wonder where the water comes from. Look up and you'll see it: the massive sandstone cliff walls show manganese stains where winter snows melt and summer monsoons flow.

Continuing through, the trail begins a right-leaning, winding ascent that turns sharply uphill for the final 90 feet. Ⓓ This takes you above the trees on the canyon floor to an open red rock hillside suitable for sitting. A sign here indicates the end of the trail. What it doesn't indicate is that the tempting boulder above it is pure danger.

It cannot be climbed, and at least one person who tried wound up dead from a fall.

Take a safer route by heading across and up from the sign to the natural bench in the red rocks. It's the perfect place to look wide over the canyon you've walked, and look up and out to the majestic walls above.

The Return Route

On the way back, you'll be pleasantly surprised by how much more you can see, despite being on the same route. The views through "Bowling Alley" are great, as are those of the high walls leading out of the canyon. Surer of your footing and, with your eyes newly opened, you'll be able to take in a lot more of what is around you.

The odds of passing through the resort's rear entry are slim to none, as the gate lock has been improved and there is little to grab onto if you had jumping over in mind. I'd stick to the trail instead, knowing you have exactly one mile to go.

If you've got enough energy, you can attempt the short Vista Trail as a final addition. The uphill trail winds around to the back of Kachina Woman. Most interesting here is the view out over the Red Rock–Secret Mountain Wilderness toward Sedona, looking over the low, green piñon-juniper forest.

As Long as You're Here Don't take getting into Enchantment Resort for granted. Most of the year, you can't. I recommend you call 928-282-2900 and make reservations for Tii Gavo (the grill) with the balcony views. To really live it up, plan ahead, and follow an early Sunday walk with brunch at the resort's Yavapai Restaurant.

Visit Palatki Ruin by taking Boynton Pass Road (FR 152C). Follow it for 4 miles, (it turns to a passable dirt road after a mile) then turn right onto 795 for 1.8 miles to the parking lot. A Red Rock Pass will get you in, and here you'll find both ancient dwellings and pictographs. Call 282-3854 for reservations .

West Sedona

Hiking Time:
1 hour, 10 minutes
for the roundtrip.

30 to 40 minutes up and
less than that to return.

Trail Length:
2 miles roundtrip.

Elevation Change:
362 feet up.
Trailhead is 4,598 feet, and
the bridge is 4,960 feet.

Devil's Bridge

Without a long drive or a lengthy trail, you can find yourself in the midst of natural wonders in under an hour.

THE TRAIL TO DEVIL'S BRIDGE IS A short but hearty uphill hike. Just a mile in length, it ends at a dramatic natural arch that's great for photo-taking. A couple of steep stairs keep those with vertigo or an extreme fear of heights off this trail, but for everyone else, it's a quick jaunt to spectacular scenery.

Devil's Bridge is a perfect example of why hiking in Sedona is such a lucky adventure. Without a long drive or a lengthy trail, you can find yourself in the midst of natural wonders in under an hour. Whether you take the steep parts slowly or race all the way to the top, you can be home to see the photos in no time at all.

When your desire for adventure is great but time is short, try Devil's Bridge.

Driving Directions From the "Y," take 89A west for 3 miles, and turn right at the stoplight onto Dry Creek Road. Drive two miles to Forest Road 152. Note that this sign mentions Vultee Arch and other trails, but not Devil's Bridge. It's a rough dirt road, but any passenger car will do fine if you take your time. Don't stop until you've gone 1.3 miles (at under 10 miles an hour, that's at least 10 minutes) reaching a small sign on the right pointing into the parking lot. The trail begins by the sign "Devil's Bridge #120" at the front of the lot. The drive takes about 25 minutes from Uptown, depending on how fast you like to drive on dirt.

Trail Notes

• No restrooms. The closest would be back out on Hwy 89A at the Giant gas station and convenience store.
• Though the Forest Service lists this trail as "easy," it is all uphill, and at 4,500 feet of altitude the air can feel a little thin.
• The stone stairs up top can be scary for folks without a good sense of balance, not to mention the bridge itself.
• Pleasant anytime of year, although the sun comes up late here, meaning it can be chilly on winter mornings. Also, tricky stairs don't make this the best trail if conditions are inclement. Treacherous in winter.
• Please be careful if you do walk out along the bridge. The Forest Service recommends against it.
• Official name: DEVIL'S BRIDGE, #120.

Devils Bridge Trail

This trail is ridiculously easy to follow at the beginning and absurdly difficult at the end. On a recent visit, I noticed that everyone was trying to find their own route up. Unfortunately, only one way works. This is the one.

The ease of the trail at its beginning comes from its width; in fact, it was originally a Jeep road. Ⓐ Today it is open only for hikers, so you don't have to worry about SUVs, horses or mountain bikers. Above and to your left tower panels of red rock, striped by manganese. It takes more than a thousand years for this mineral to form from the reaction of the iron in the red rock with rainwater. Above and

to the right you'll see Balanced Rock, which looks even more amazing farther up the trail. Ⓑ Within 10 minutes, at about three-tenths of a mile along the way, the trail will begin

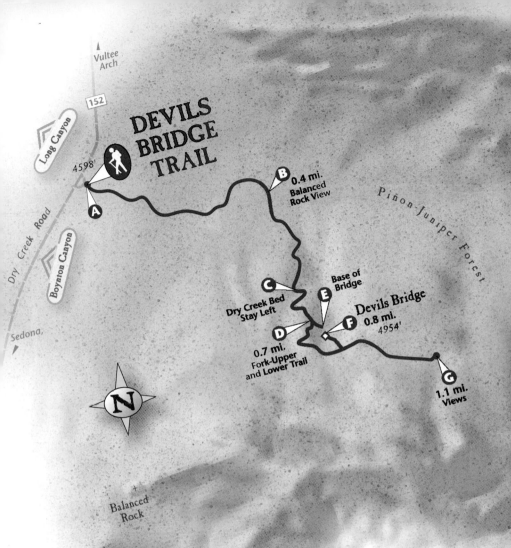

Vultee
Arch

152

Long Canyon

4598'

DEVILS BRIDGE TRAIL

B 0.4 mi.
Balanced
Rock View

Piñon-Juniper Forest

A

Dry Creek Road

Boynton Canyon

Sedona,

C
Dry Creek Bed
Stay Left

Base of
Bridge

E

Devils Bridge
F 0.8 mi.
4954'

D

0.7 mi.
Fork-Upper
and Lower Trail

G
1.1 mi.
Views

N

Balanced
Rock

curving to the right, turning upward toward the north face of Capitol Butte, also known as Thunder Mountain and previously known as Grayback. There are plenty more peaks in Sedona whose names have changed or who have no name at all. Find one you like, and come up with your own name!

There are only two points where you need to make certain of the trail. After 15 to 20 minutes of walking (about half a mile), the trail turns upward and to the left, but you may be tempted to walk through the dry creek bed to the right. **C** The logs resting there are designed to stop you. That's exactly what you should do, because the creek bed leads nowhere.

WHY IS SEDONA SO GREEN?

If you're coming from somewhere other than the Southwest, then most of Sedona's forests probably won't match your vision of the term. With the exception of Oak Creek Canyon, Sedona rests primarily in an ecological zone known as Piñon-Juniper Forest. The term derives from the two primary evergreens here.

Piñon pines are short, hardy trees whose cones produce tasty nuts every second autumn.

Juniper trees come in a few varieties, including *Utah* and *Alligator,* the latter easily identified by crocodilian bark.

Bluish juniper "berries" are hardly tasty, but were typically soaked in hot water by native peoples, which reduced the bitterness. The stringy bark was often used as bedding for children's cradles, while the wood could be used to make digging sticks for agriculture.

Together, these stout trees cover Red Rock Country, steadfastly surviving heat and drought. They've learned not to expect rain, and therefore, prefer to stay small, reducing their dependence on water.

The second point comes at seven-tenths of a mile, where the trail forks. On your right you'll pass a large boulder and a red rock face overhead. Cairns (the red rock piles we use to mark a trail) mark a narrow path dropping off to the left, leading to the base of the arch. Ⓓ If you're tired and have had enough climbing, take this route. Otherwise, follow ahead and to the right, on the main trail. Here you'll find a set of rock steps to climb up the cliff face. They aren't extremely difficult, but the lack of a railing makes some people nervous.

Rest for a moment at the small plateau-like overlook and take a look around. Ⓔ In the distance, look for a small group of houses on a hillside. The ridge with houses on its side was once the famous Rachel's Knoll, a space donated for contemplation and meditation. Sadly, the space has now been developed: Rachel's kids sold it.

The final portion of the trail leads away from the overlook, up and then to the left (east). In just a couple of minutes you'll emerge to look out at Devil's Bridge. If you've got children with you, I recommend taking hold of their hands before the bridge is visible, which will make you all feel safer when you come upon it.

Hopefully, you won't have used up all your pictures by the time you arrive, because you can get some wonderful photos here. Ⓕ For the very best shot of all, have your partner stand on the bridge while you shoot from slightly higher up on the mountainside, capturing your loved one along with the bridge and the views of the Red Rock–Secret Mountain Wilderness.

If you desire to go a bit farther, the trail does continue on, heading east from the foot of the bridge. However, the trail is not well marked and it has no specific destination. Still, if you've brought a picnic with you, it is nice to get away from the bridge if there's a crowd.

The other option is to head down to the trail that leads under the bridge. It is never crowded, and the view up to the bridge is impressive. Ⓖ To get there, return down the main trail and take the right turn that comes after you descend the final rock staircase.

As Long as You're Here World-class Enchantment Resort can be reached by driving further on the paved Dry Creek Road and turning left at the first stop sign. Follow the road two miles, and turn right at the second stop sign staying on paved roads the entire way. Note that you will need reservations to get in, so call ahead (928-282-2900) to have a drink and a bite at the Tii Gavo grill or the Yavapai Restaurant.

West Sedona

Hiking Time:
1 hour, 30 minutes
for the roundtrip, or bring
a picnic and stay longer.

Trail Length:
2.5 miles
for the roundtrip.

Only 0.7 mile to mesa top.

Elevation Change:
410 feet up,
all in one smooth zig-zag
from the start of the trail.

Doe Mesa

A long, winding zig-zag will get you up to the top without too much effort.

S OMETIMES YOU JUST GET LUCKY. To my mind, Doe Mesa is lucky from a hiker's point of view, a place where a moderate climb leads to fantastic views. As you pause at the beginning to take a look at the hill before you, you may ask yourself, "How the heck are we going to get up that?" Don't worry, the trail, although hidden in the brush so well that you can't see it, is actually a long, winding zig-zag that will get you up to the top without too much effort.

Don't take Doe for granted though. The physical effort required is matched by a need for mental concentration. In other words: watch your step. While nearby Devil's Bridge offers a single spectacular landmark to watch, Doe doesn't give you any one thing to look at. Instead the views are varied and expansive: you'll want to take it all in.

Doe is the trail that will make you think about which friends back home you'll try to talk into coming back to see it. Beware: on reflection, Doe may become the trail you never want to share.

Trail Notes

- There are no restrooms here. Your closest option is the environmental toilets at the Boynton Canyon trailhead.
- Photographers should note shots of the north ridge as you rise. Aim for lizards and plants once on top. Save film for far side of the mesa to shoot the sheer cliffs and distant peaks.
- Doe Mesa is ideal to walk in any season. My only hesitancy would be on spring afternoons, when the rim is exposed to strong winds.
- Official name: DOE MOUNTAIN, #60.

Doe Mesa Trail

We call it Doe Mesa because it is as much a mesa as you can find here. Doe is steep up the sides and perfectly flat on top. At least, it's as flat as Mother Nature makes them around here.

Although you are probably anxious to begin the climb, it is worth taking your time in the opening paces of the trail. Ⓑ What we in the Southwest would consider a meadow is full of interesting features that most people miss. The wildflowers of spring (in some years, this has been a purple carpet of owl clover), the yuccas and cacti of summer offer unexpected color. Soon enough you'll arrive at the sign-up box, which is always worth utilizing.

Doe is about to bring you up gently, and you can stop at as many zigs and zags as you want on the way up. From nonstop to constant stopping, it's your choice. Take as much time to catch your breath as you need, and quickly you'll be surprised to see your car in the parking lot, appearing small and far away.

Higher up, the trail brings you further across the southwest side of the mesa. When you've gone as far across that side of the mountain as you can, stop to enjoy the views. Ⓒ As you look over north to the parking lot again, massive Bear Mountain now reveals more of itself.

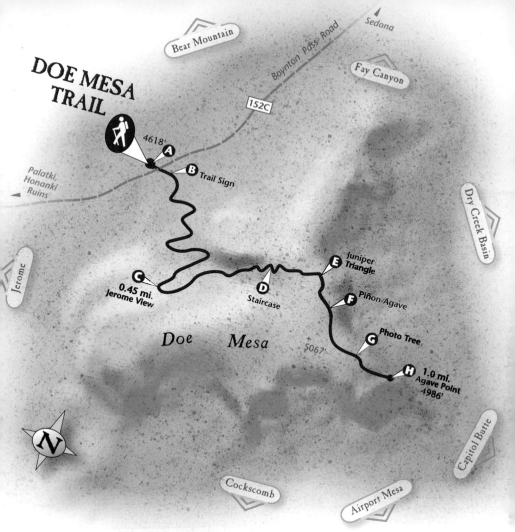

To the west you can see Mingus Mountain in the distance. Look closer and you'll notice, halfway up Mingus, the old mining town of Jerome. During its heyday, more than 15,000 populated "The Billion Dollar Copper Camp," as this Western boomtown was known. On the hill above the town you can make out a thin white letter "J."

The walk from this end of the mesa across to the other is a delightful 0.2 mile. This flat portion allows you to enjoy the views with ease. In fact, coming across you'll get some particularly good photos. The best shots are those aimed to include the nearby wall whose hollowed-out portions appear man-made. They're not, nor is anything else you can see here. Just the wonders of water and wind, multiplied by millions of years.

Once you've come all the way across, the trail leads you up the final short climb to the rim. After 25 to 45 minutes of walking (just under 0.7 mile), the entry to the top of the mesa is a narrow red rock chute. It's best to use both hands to climb through. **(D)** Step out of the chute to the left, avoid the cairns to the right, and continue uphill. Ahead is a very tall cairn. When you get to it, there is one very important thing to do: stop and look around. First, this gives you a chance to rest and celebrate. Second, it offers an opportunity to plan what comes next.

Though the mesa is so flat that it isn't physically challenging, it is easy to lose your way up here. That wastes your effort and destroys

ANCIENT RUINS

From approximately A.D. 700-1400, the culture we know as the Sinagua inhabited this region. The Sinagua combined hunting, gathering and agriculture to support themselves, and built masonry dwellings in the canyons. Their trade routes extended for hundreds of miles until changes including drought contibuted to the Sinagua's departure. The Hopi Indians claim that the Sinagua joined their ancestors on the mesas to the north, though many likely stayed behind, intermarrying with the Yavapai.

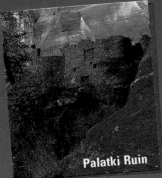
Palatki Ruin

PALATKI: In a small box canyon about 15 miles west of Sedona, the ancients painted, pecked, and inscribed some 6,000 rock art images. A cliff dwelling at the head of the canyon sheltered Sinagua villagers from A.D. 1100 to 1300. Trails leading to the rock art and ruin are less than a mile. Reservations required; call (928) 282-3854. Check road conditions during or after wet weather when sites may close due to impassible forest roads. For more information, call (928) 282-4119, or visit www.redrockcountry.org. **HONANKI:** A high-clearance vehicle is recommended to reach this site, about 20 miles west of Sedona. A short trail skirts a series of rooms built against Loy Butte. Sinagua and Yavapai painted pictographs above the masonry walls. **V-V RANCH PETROGLYPH SITE:** About 20 miles southeast of Sedona, this former ranch along Beaver Creek was once the site of Sinagua fields of maize, beans and squash. An easy 0.5 mi. trail leads to the largest petroglyph panel in the area. Open 9:30am – 3:30pm, Friday – Monday. **MONTEZUMA CASTLE:** One of the most photogenic cliff dwellings in Arizona, this five-story pueblo near Camp Verde was occupied by the Sinagua until A.D. 1400. For more information, call (928) 567-3322. **MONTEZUMA WELL:** The well, a deep sinkhole, is central to the Yavapai creation story. Sinagua pueblos overlook the waters. This oasis in the desert makes for great wildflower viewing in early spring. For more information, call (928) 567-3322. **TUZIGOOT:** This sprawling hilltop pueblo, located between Cottonwood and Clarkdale, was occupied by the Sinagua until A.D. 1400. An interpretive trail leads visitors through centuries of prehistory, and the museum displays the finest local collection of artifacts. For more information, call (928) 634-5564, or visit www.nps.gov/tuzi.

the fragile terrain. As a matter of fact, take a look around and you may find wandering souls at this very moment wishing they had gotten their bearings a bit sooner. The top of the mesa is flat and easy, so you're going to be tempted to race across. But if you do, it will be very easy to get lost and forget how to find your way back. This matters because there is no other good way down, and there are a lot of dangerous ways down that people get stuck on. So mentally mark the spot, and keep in mind how you expect to return here. Also, keep your eyes open for sharp stuff of all kinds at ankle level, from agave to prickly pear to scrub oak.

The tall cairn at the hilltop will be your guidepost. While several trails appear to be equally viable, I recommend continuing straight ahead over the top. Yes, there are strong, tall cairns built to the left and right, but these are by no means "official." Rather, it's as if a battle of cairn builders has taken place here. Many are what I call "false cairns." Sometimes they were built to mark former campsites (now illegal up here) and sometimes they were built by well-meaning individuals trying to indicate a path. The result is, it's a mess up here.

Thank goodness that some minor trail markers were added by the Forest Service (and the volunteers of Friends of the Forest) in 2006. These brown metal posts are three to four feet tall and a couple of inches wide. Nonetheless, a good description can help you get across smoothly. From the ridge directly above the chute, head east, roughly in line with the dirt road (far below) and generally in line with the chute. There will be an initial left and right turn, but generally you'll head about 150 paces straight across the mesa. That can be hard to count, especially since your attention will be taken up by how stunningly flat it is here.

You'll be tempted to continue all the way across to the other end of the mesa, especially since glimpses of panoramic views will appear above the tree-tops. Resist it, and find yourself coming to a spot in a triangle of juniper trees. Turn a sharp left and head for the tall juniper on the right. Ⓔ Moving past it, head for a piñon pine with blades of sharp yucca and beargrass next to it. Here a narrow path will take you further south, bringing you gradually out to the rim. If you can't find your way, pause to do what always works best: choose the most worn trail, and see where it takes you. Whether or not you're on the path that I recommend, take a few "mental photos" so that you'll be able to return along the same route.

One way or another, you're about to see some great views. If you've located the piñon/beargrass/yucca spot, you'll lean left to duck under another juniper and reach the rim in view of an old craggy juniper. Ⓖ If you haven't been able to follow along, then look for the craggy juniper at whichever point you come to the rim, and head that way.

This is one of my favorite spots in all of Sedona. To the left, you can see the cliff edges of the mesa, then a bit of Fay Canyon, then the buildings of Enchantment Resort in Boynton Canyon. Long Canyon and the Red Rock–Secret Mountain Wilderness follow next as you shift your glance ahead. Mescal Mountain lies in front, and that's Wilson Mountain in the background, in turn leading you to see Capitol Butte, also known as Thunder Mountain. It's a great place to take a photo, particularly if you use the old juniper in the foreground of the frame.

From here, there's still more to see, especially parts few people get to. In fact, I'd say that of all those who attempt Doe Mesa, the overwhelming majority never get this far. Either because they've under-estimated the climb or because they're unaware of the views that await them, they stop as they arrive at the mesa and simply turn and go back.

Lucky you. Now your choice is simply between the thrill of walking along the ridge and the security of staying further back. The former is the obvious choice: just stay a few feet back from the rim, and test the rocks as you cross them. A good rule of thumb: the bigger the rock, the more likely it is to be secure.

The latter option dictates turning away from the views and walking 14 paces forward from the craggy juniper. On the left you'll see a

narrow path. Follow this path or walk the rim for another five minutes and you'll come to the mesa's spectacular southeast corner. (H) Hopefully the new Aerie development won't make you want to turn around. In addition to your views of the Red Rock–Secret Mountain Wilderness and Capitol Butte, you can now add this view of Airport Mesa, with Munds and Lee mountains behind it. Courthouse Butte is the lone monolith in the distance; Bell Rock appears demure to its right. Cathedral Rock appears to have wings sticking out behind it: that's actually a different formation called The Transept or Seven Sisters. Those with good eyes can spy the green-roofed buildings of Sedona Red Rock High School. With really, really good eyes, you can look below the high school and find the patches of dirt and wooden-barrel frame of the Sedona Cultural Park. The dirt indicates parking lots; the frame is the structure above the stage at the amphitheatre, a 5,000-seat performance venue. Far to the west is Mingus Mountain, with the town of Cottonwood below it.

The Return Route

Having confidently arrived at the top, you may feel comfortable enough to walk by the eastern ridge on your return. There's no need to do it if it scares you; however, the potential photographs are great. In particular, look for shadows on the ridges below, and on the distant cliff walls of Fay, Boynton and Long canyons.

Try your best to return along the same route, in order to preserve nature. If you have problems, simply head west, and make certain not to head downhill until you find the proper cairns. Find the narrow chute that you came up for the safe way down.

As Long as You're Here The Palatki Ruin features both ancient dwellings and pictographs. Pop out the cell phone and call 282-3854 to get a spot on their limited schedule. From the trail parking lot, continue west for three miles on Boynton Pass Road/152C until it ends. Turn right onto 795, and follow the signs. You'll arrive in less than two more miles. Returning via Boynton Pass Road/152C, take a left onto the paved road to visit Enchantment Resort. Reward yourself with a drink at Tii Gavo (the grill) or Yavapai Restaurant, but note that you need reservations. Call ahead to 928-282-2900.

Uptown Sedona

Hiking Time:
3 hours, 25 minutes
for the round-trip.
About 55 minutes to the
mesa top. Just over an hour
from the final overlook
back to the parking lot.

Trail Length:
5 miles
for the roundtrip.

Elevation Change:
914 feet up.
Trailhead is 4,541 feet,
you'll pass 5,070 feet at the
mesa, and reach 5,455 feet
at the final overlook.

*B*rins *M*esa

**If you like great views on a
moderate hike that gets your
lungs pumping, this trail
may be perfect for you.**

B RINS MESA IS A DELIGHTFUL TRAIL that combines warm down-in-the-canyon feelings with the thrill of high-above-it-all vistas. The trick is getting from one to the other, which makes this trail a serious but rewarding workout.

Although the trail begins just a mile from the crowds of Uptown Sedona, it is unlikely that you'll run into more than a few people during your outing. Even if they somehow stumbled here, three nearby trailheads would succeed in distracting them, leaving Brins Mesa to you. The trail seduces you to move along the gentle canyon floor. By the time you come to the canyon wall, curiosity to see what's there will overcome the strain of climbing it. You won't be disappointed.

A summer wildfire in 2006 scorched some of the mesa, but has only made the scenery more fascinating. If you like great views on a moderate hike that gets your lungs pumping, this trail may be perfect for you.

Driving Directions From the "Y," head north on Hwy 89A toward Uptown Sedona. At 0.3 mile, just beyond the stoplight at Forest Road, use the left turn lane to turn onto Jordan Road. Follow it directly into the Jordan Park development, then turn left at the stop sign onto Park Ridge Drive. Continue through the cul-de-sac which you will exit from over a rounded curb onto a roadway above. It turns to dirt and you'll soon see a sign for several trails: Jim Thompson, Brins Mesa and two newer ones, Jordan and Cibola. The road has some deep holes, so drive gently, and make sure to continue to the end of the dirt road. Please park head on, in a way that doesn't impede others leaving or arriving. Although the map on the board refers to the Jim Thompson Trail, this is the right place.

Trail Notes

• There is no restroom here. The closest public restroom would be among the Uptown shops.
• Ideal in all seasons. The mesa can be soggy in winter if there has been rain or snow, but that also means there can be waterfalls in the corner behind Earth Angel Spire.
• Official name: BRINS MESA, #119.

Brins Mesa Trail

Changes in 2002 created a new parking lot here, allowing hikers to start this trail closer into the wilderness. This means you'll be in the car as you pass the Jordan, Cibola Pass and Jim Thompson trailheads, which should help keep you from choosing those tempting but less exciting routes.

Just a minute ahead, the hike starts out on gravel. Then, you'll pass through a knee-high fence designed to separate the natural area from the cars.

The trail officially begins here and points you straight at The Mitten, a beautiful hand-shaped formation. Ⓐ (Okay, so a true mitten has a thumb, not a pinkie, too.) This is a perfect spot to photograph the rock, especially as it catches sunlight in the morning. However, this canyon has beauty to show you no matter what time of day and there are many good formations on the other side of the canyon that are best photographed in the afternoon. The first mile is the gentlest rise of the hike, you'll gain 150 feet as the canyon welcomes you in. If the trail were a Stairmaster machine, this would be the gentle warm-up.

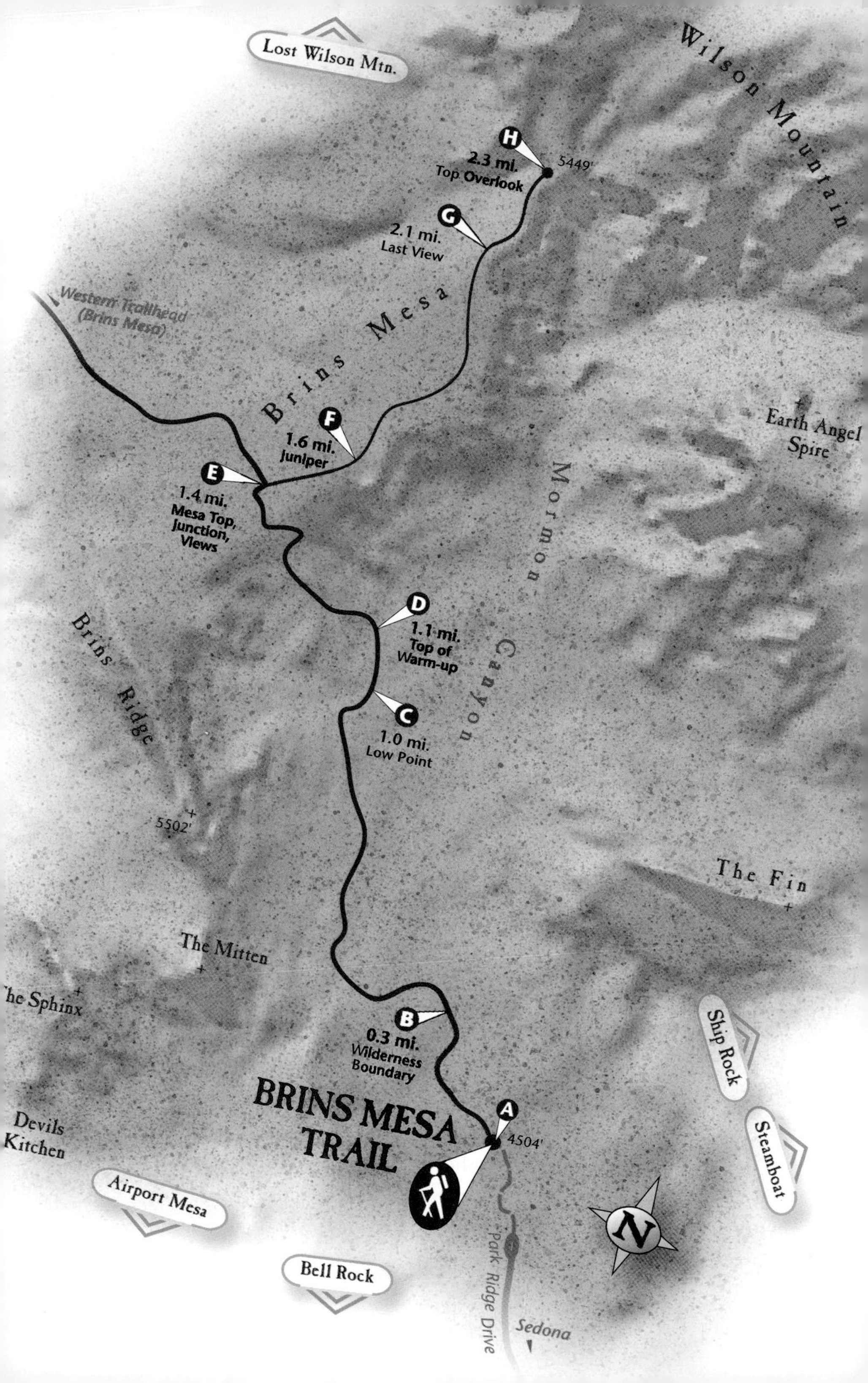

Lost Wilson Mtn.

Wilson Mountain

H
2.3 mi.
Top Overlook
5449'

G
2.1 mi.
Last View

Western Trailhead
(Brins Mesa)

Brins Mesa

Earth Angel
Spire

F
1.6 mi.
Juniper

E
1.4 mi.
Mesa Top,
Junction,
Views

Mormon
Canyon

D 1.1 mi.
Top of
Warm-up

Brins Ridge

C
1.0 mi.
Low Point

5502'

The Fin

The Mitten

The Sphinx

B
0.3 mi.
Wilderness
Boundary

Ship Rock

A
4504'

Steamboat

BRINS MESA
TRAIL

Devils
Kitchen

Airport Mesa

Park Ridge Drive

N

Bell Rock

Sedona

At 0.3 miles, you'll pass a small sign indicating that you are entering "Wilderness." Ⓑ I think it is important to explain what that means. It is an area within the National Forest where bicycles and motorized vehicles are restricted. Which brings me to another question, namely, how well protected are our public lands? The short answer is "Not very." National Forest can be traded away to those who, for example, would offer land in exchange. National Monuments are a bit better protected. National Parks such as the Grand Canyon are the best protected, but even these can be developed for recreation and tourism. My point? Red Rock Country is worth preserving, but it won't happen automatically. It takes

awareness and action, and trails like this provide all the motivation.

The views to your east (on your right side) are impressive too. The long diagonal formation is Ship Rock, and to its right is the smokestack of Steamboat Rock. Meanwhile, the straightaway in front of you shows the work of Friends of the Forest, a local volunteer group. Here you can see that a wide trail has been narrowed by branches and sticks, designed to keep you in a small chute. Try to walk the center of the trail, which greatly reduces damage.

Twenty minutes along, the trail will head due east and you'll begin to feel as if you are tucked into the canyon. Depending upon which portion of the trail you're on, Mormon Canyon will fill the northern (left) side of this view.

Twenty-five to thirty minutes along, the trail feels about jeep-width, and you'll realize that you're not really walking along the floor of the canyon. To the right you'll catch glimpses of the floor, and you'll begin to feel yourself rising. By now you've got a clear view of the back wall of this canyon that you are headed toward. Looking at it you might ask, where's the mesa? It's on top, and you're about to begin the uphill climb to get to it.

Just a few minutes further ahead the S-curve the trail takes will reveal some giant manzanita. Most manzanitas are shrubs only two to three feet tall, but these tower over your head. Stroke the beautiful, smooth wood to appreciate it. It's also a good marker for the only possible wrong turn you'll be tempted to make. Just ahead the trail appears to fork. The rising left-hand side is your choice, and the views are about to improve significantly. You are now at 4,700 feet, and this is where the air will begin to feel a little thin if you're not from these parts. Ⓒ

You're about to enter the Stairmaster's next stage: the vigorous warm-up. Although less than 70 feet up, it's likely to get anyone breathing hard. At its crest, the trail turns sharply right. Before you continue on, I'd suggest a rest stop here, where you can sit on a pleasant red rock ridge to your left. However, this area may be camouflaged in an effort to keep people going in the right direction. If so, take a seat at the top of the staircase you've just climbed. Ⓓ

Ah, views. I love 'em! But what I love even more is to know they're going to get better! So once you've caught your breath and had some water, take on the real Stairmaster and continue uphill where your challenge awaits. The trail now takes you directly to the mesa. One hundred feet higher, the spires below Wilson Mountain become more evident. Beyond the long-dead log bordering the trail's right side, you've got a fine photo spot. Successive ridge lines create wonderful layers of depth, and the tall walls of Mormon Canyon are the perfect backdrop.

Climbing higher now, the piñon pines and juniper trees cover the canyon floor like wall-to-wall carpet. You can also see Camel's Head from a new angle. As you notice an old wire fence to the right, the trail becomes very rocky, requiring as much mental concentration to place your feet as it takes physical effort. You've got another 100 feet to go.

"Expert Time" to the mesa would be less than an hour, but I think the real experts are the ones who take their time to enjoy. Having

PLANT OF THE CENTURY

Among the most interesting of Southwestern plants is the agave, known locally as century plant. Although it looks like an aloe vera to many visitors, it is entirely different. It won't live a full century (a misconception leading to its nickname), but it can live decades, at the end of which something astonishing happens. Out of the center of the plant a stalk will grow up several inches each day, until reaching a remarkable height of up to 20 feet. At that point, the local variety opens to display beautiful golden blossoms.

The plant dies from the bottom up and loses it color similarly. Look around and you'll probably see plants from a prior year that are now brown-gray in color. Yet even once dead, the plant aptly represents the Greek roots for its name: agavos means "illustrious."

Native people used the leaves' sharp points as needles and fiber from the leaves to make sandals. In addition, they could harvest and roast the fleshy "heart" of the agave. Roasting pits are found near pictograph and petroglyph sites in Sedona, suggesting that this nutritious food was consumed during special occasions.

Like other succulents, agaves can store water as an adaptation to dry climates. The local agave is cousin to the blue agave (the source of tequila). Be very careful around agaves. Their leaves are sharp and spiky, with tips that can pierce like like a dagger.

come this far—a little over 500 feet up in a little less than a mile and a half—you've got a few choices to make now. (E) First, you can continue across the mesa on the main trail, which leads you back into the Red-Rock–Secret Mountain Wilderness, completing the three-mile trail at a parking lot and trailhead to the north, off a rough dirt road. Second, you can stop and relax here before turning around. I recommend the third option. Take a hard right turn and find that the mesa's surprises are only beginning.

Across Brins Mesa

This is the kind of place that causes proud Sedonans to suggest that when we die and go to heaven, it will be a parallel move. Heading north toward Wilson Mountain, there are great views to the right. There is also unexpected beauty on the left. Through the spring, the meadow can be covered with yellow asters, purple verbena, red penstemons and orange Indian paintbrush. In the summertime these give way to prickly pear cactus blooms and century plants towering toward the sky. Winter can be chilly up here, but the deep blue sky will keep you from noticing the cold.

If you head off to the right up along the mesa, the views improve. One hundred feet along the path, Bell Rock becomes visible in the distance, while the rock a friend calls "The Trailer Hitch" stands out within the canyon. It's a good name: maybe it will stick.

The mesa's name makes good sense to cattlemen. Here a brindle bull roamed freely, once upon a time, and the abbreviation for its color—"brin"—was applied to the mesa. Like Marg's Draw and Bear Mountain, it is a place where the animals, not humans are commemorated by name.

A few pointers come into play to continue this adventure. The trails across the mesa are narrow and are not particularly well marked. What's more, the views are so great it's easy to forget to pay attention. It's okay: almost any route will get you there, but staying to the left moves you along more quickly. In fact, look for the first split in the trail at a juniper tree. (F) It stands on your left, 0.2 mile from where you first reached the mesa. On my last visit, a small prickly pear cactus divided the paths. Go left here, backing away from the edge. This will take you away from the views, but lead you to much better ones.

In another five minutes you may begin saying to yourself, "I thought mesas were supposed to be flat!" Consider this gentle rise to be the Stairmaster's cool-down. At each of the next two-tenths of a mile, you'll keep veering left when the trail offers a choice. The views keep getting better until you part from the rim, and you can see the buildings on top of the truly flat Airport Mesa in the distance, with Cathedral Rock rising out behind it. Three-quarters of a mile (about 35 to 40 minutes) from the start of the mesa, you'll give up these views entirely. Ⓖ

The trail narrows in its final stretch to the end of the mesa, and it is real easy to get yourself scratched up here. Take your time and watch your step as you negotiate past yuccas and scrub oaks. As the trail dips over the north side of the mesa, the lost views of Sedona are replaced by new ones of the Red Rock-Secret Mountain Wilderness. Far off, you can perhaps see a small home on a hillside. Above that home was once the sanctuary known as Rachel's Knoll, a private space open for visitors to walk a trail, see a medicine wheel and meditate in a beautiful spot. Long Canyon extends beyond the knoll, and Boynton Canyon is off to its left.

You'll negotiate your way around the side of the mesa until you find yourself facing a beautiful red cliff wall. When the path turns to red dirt, step up to the right and follow east toward Wilson Mountain, up and forward over the rocks. Pausing, you'll see that you can walk right up the red rocks until…jackpot! A nice flat red rock, with another, higher place to sit on the end.

What to call this place? "Celebration Point"? "Brins Beach"? Perhaps you'll name it after yourself just for the day. At 5,455 feet, you've walked 2.3 miles, which wouldn't sound like much on the high school track back home. But where will you find two and a third prettier miles? Ⓗ On rare occasions, Angel Falls flows in a split in the deep interior of the canyon, particularly in late winter when overnight snowfalls can be followed by warm sunny days.

The views are truly outstanding. In fact, they are among the juiciest rewards to any trail I know, and I know a lot of them! If you face northeast, you're looking at Wilson Mountain. Look for the dark cliff edge that appears quite different from the blonde and red sandstone below. This is lava, which flowed less than ten million years ago, and covered the underlying sandstone. As a result, this formation resisted erosion better than other nearby ridges, and stands today as Sedona's tallest peak at 7,122 feet.

To the southeast you can pick out among the spires one called Earth Angel. Can you see an angel with a halo and wings held in tight and forward? To the southwest, in the distance, you're looking at a ridge that stretches from behind Coffee Pot Rock, although it is out of view. Turning your head slightly toward the south, you'll see Cathedral Rock sticking up above Airport Mesa. Yup, it's a genuine airport, although nothing bigger than a private jet takes off here. Ten degrees north of west is the Seven Canyons area. If the greenery looks a little too perfect, that's because it's a golf course.

Retrace your steps carefully to find your way back onto the path. On the way home, you'll see faces in the rocks around The Mitten. From the vista point, you can see the Camel's Head and back.

As Long as You're Here Brins Mesa shows how close you can be to Uptown Sedona, and yet how far away. Just a couple of minutes from the bustle, you'll find great solitude. Nonetheless, once you've climbed, go enjoy some bustle!

For a cultural stop, the Sedona Heritage Museum is new and interesting, particularly its features on Sedona's Hollywood history. It's a great place to learn more about pioneers like Jim Thompson, for whom the nearby trail was the road home!

Along Jordan Road you'll find all the food choices you'll need. Once you turn onto it from 89A, look for the small Sally's Grill on the right for the best ribs in town. I like beginning across the street and slightly further up at Sedona Memories Bakery & Cafe for the best sandwiches for my picnic. You can also consider Takashi on the left for tonight's dinner.

Out on the main drag, Oaxaca (Wa-HA-k) offers Mexican food, and the Canyon Breeze offers beer. For fine dining with a Southwestern influence, check out the Cowboy Club. Or perhaps you'd like to go straight to dessert? Try the Black Cow Café for tasty ice cream.

Uptown Sedona

Hiking Time:
3 hours for the roundtrip to the creek and back.

Trail Length:
4.9 miles for the roundtrip from the Schnebly Hill trailhead to the second creek crossing and back.

Elevation Change:
223 feet down.
The high point on the ridge near the trailhead is 4,535 feet and the low point at the creek is 4,312 feet.

Huckaby Trail

Hillside and creek, evergreens and leaves, city views and wilderness—Huckaby has it all.

THE DAY I FIRST HIKED THE NEW Huckaby Trail, I felt like a child with a brand new Christmas toy. A beautifully crafted trail, Huckaby offers views and surprises; hills and valleys and red rocks; and a chance to get close to the water.

This is a trail that is more vigorous than long, winding along with its dips and ascents to provide you with new perspectives of Red Rock Country. Although the town and its traffic are visible from the trail, there are wonderful long-distance vistas. If you can't get a lift or park a second car at the far end, then make sure you have the time and the energy to walk out. I bet you will: like a good workout, Huckaby will stretch you, not kill you.

Close to the heart of town, Huckaby offers the best of Sedona in a nice, healthy package. If you don't want to choose between hillside and creek, evergreens and leaves, city views and wilderness, then pick Huckaby and you'll get it all.

Driving Directions To get here you'll want to locate Schnebly Hill Road, which veers off Hwy 179 just over the bridge past the Tlaquepaque shopping village as you head south. Heading north on Hwy 179, you'll veer right onto Schnebly 0.25 mile beyond the Hillside galleries. The road begins about 0.3 mile below the "Y" intersection of Hwy 179 and Hwy 89A. Follow it until the pavement ends, with the parking lot and trailhead to your left.

Trail Notes

- There are toilets at the trailhead on Schnebly Hill, and none at Midgely Bridge.
- Hills on the trail make for about 350 feet of ascent in each direction. In other words, this trail is a perfect example of how elevation change alone doesn't give you a sense of the effort.
- A great trail for warm weather. You may want to bring sandals and swimwear to take enjoy the water.
- Although away from the crowds, the trail yields views of the city that may or may not be enticing to you, depending upon the kind of solitude you seek.
- Official Name: HUCKABY TRAIL, #161.

Huckaby Trail

If you're going to get lost on Huckaby Trail, it's right at the start. So pay attention. Standing at the kiosk where Red Rock Passes are sold, avoid heading for the picnic tables over to the right. Ⓐ Instead, walk straight ahead and follow this curvy portion of the trail. People camped here at one time before the parking lot and the trail existed. Just because something has been trodden upon doesn't mean it's the trail.

Curiously, the trail description on one of the boards lists this as an "easy" trail, while the chart listing all trails in the area refers to it as "moderate." The first description is flat-out wrong. Watch for the small brown trail sign as you admire an abundance of vegetation. On a spring day I saw orange globemallow flowers and purple-colored blue dicks (honest, that's their name) along with diminutive sumac, piñon pine and juniper trees.

The views begin almost immediately. In front of you is Capitol Butte, with the spire known as Chimney Rock beside it. The Cockscomb is somewhat obscured. After a few minutes of walking you'll see a Huckaby sign indicating that you follow straight ahead. The Marg's Draw trail heads left, crossing the paved road that you drove in on and that is now parallel to you as you walk.

Trail finding is easier now thanks to the stone piles enclosed by wire known as *cairns*. Pronounced kar-en, like the woman's name, it is typical of trail markers in the region. While in most parts of the country where trails are marked with a blaze—usually, a notch in the tree bark—here we have open areas with no trees at all. Informal cairns (without the wire) are effective, but they present two problems. First, they're easy to knock down. Second, they're easy to build! The latter is a problem when well-intentioned but inexperienced hikers think they've found a trail that they'd like to mark better for the rest of us. Usually, however, they've only lost their way, and the cairn merely reinforces their error.

After eight minutes of walking, prepare for a steep downhill as you turn right (north). If you pause to look across to the next hillside, you can see where you'll wind up, but first it's 70 feet downhill to the normally dry creek bed of Bear Wallow Canyon. Only in spring, when the snow melts above, are you likely to find water here.

Crossing the creek bed, you'll begin to climb. It is here that Huckaby Trail starts to strut its stuff. You see, the Forest Service and the wonderful Friends of the Forest volunteer group (who did so much of the grunt work) really seem to have thought this one through. They designed a trail that winds in a way such that all sides of Sedona are revealed to you as you go. There's no need to strain your neck on this trail: all the red rocks will be presenting themselves to you in due course.

Continuing your climb, look back east toward the early parts of the trail, and you'll now be able to see Snoopy Rock (see photo). I am always reminded of Charles Schulz, Snoopy's creator. Imagine how important creativity was to a man who died the day after his last strip was published. Now that's the way I want to go. To walk my last hike someday, soaking up my last views when I'm about 132 years old, say "thank you" and slip on to the great big mountain range in the sky.

Not everyone is lucky enough to live that long. On your right, you'll come to a bench dedicated to a local youth who lived fast and not long enough. The inscription reads: "Spirit is what you create. It's your signature on your soul. Your stamp on life. In loving memory, JOSHUA SETH WILLIAMS, 1977-1999." It is a nice place to sit, catch your breath and be grateful for what you've got. Ⓑ

Schnebly Hill Road appears nestled among the very impressive Schnebly Hill formation. The road was made in 1902, and some people say it hasn't gotten one bit better. Muddy, snowy or dusty as can be, it would take those early Sedona settlers two days to reach Flagstaff.

Small logs set into the trail prevent erosion and provide you with a nice set of steps as you continue higher. In summer the clusters of hedgehog cactus found on either side of the trail sprouts magenta flowers. White banana yucca and yellow prickly pear blossoms are also plentiful along the trail in summer.

The view past Josh Williams' bench is to the red rock Mooses Ridge. Then, as the trail turns west, there are more beautiful views. One lucky Sunday morning I could see five hot air balloons in the distance.

Admire the panorama. Starting from the south, you first see the Twin Buttes, with a saddle between them. The right side of that formation is often called Elephant Rock...can you see the trunk? Cathedral Rock is next, then the flat-topped Airport Mesa. Then the town of Sedona. There are lots of ocotillo up here—a most unusual plant that produces tiny leaves along its spiny wands after any significant rainfall. Down below you can now see Oak Creek as you come to the trail's highest point. © Chimney Rock, tall Capitol Butte and The Mitten are in the distance.

One of Sedona's more well-known critters is the javelina (hav-uh-LEE-na). It looks like a cross between a pig and a boar, but in fact it is neither. It's true name is collared pecary *(pecari tajacu)* and these animals move in small packs.

Javelina take absolutely no mind of the fact that people don't think them pretty: they're too busy eatin'! They'll turn over vegetation looking for roots to chew on, and they love the cactus pads and fruits of the prickly pear. "But what about those sharp spines?" you ask. They eat them, too.

Javelina

Javelinas' outstanding sense of smell substitutes for their poor eyesight. When it's danger that they scent, they go into action, clicking their tusks and scratching their hoofs, a sign of alertness. Usually, given an exit route, javelinas will turn tail as fast as possible.

Mule deer

Nice views of the cliffs reveal sandstone with black-colored manganese. The flood-plain of Oak Creek is below you now, and you can see all of Uptown and spy the passing tourists on Hwy 89A. Over the next several minutes, more of Sedona's lodges and service-providers appear. Among them is Therapy on the Rocks, home of massage therapist John Barnes and his team. The domed building tucked into the small canyon is the Sedona Healing Center. The Red Rock Lodge is an inexpensive place to stay. More luxurious is the Wishing Well B&B, up on the hill, where guests can enjoy a hot tub under the stars.

At 1.3 miles, you'll notice a dramatic change in the trees. You've entered a burn area, site of a small wildfire a few years ago. Ⓓ Although the charred trees demonstrate the damage, chances are you may see the new growth of wildflowers, such as purple-colored verbena.

Other than the misidentification of this trail as "easy" by the Forest Service, I've only ever heard one complaint about Huckaby, and that is that it is "too urban." Fortunately, as your path curves forward and around, you come to a view that shows off the best work of nature and of humans. Above is Wilson Mountain, and the smooth hill to its right is The Bench. Oak Creek is down below, in a nice line heading straight toward Midgely Bridge.

You're about to begin a long downhill stretch from a point roughly at the same altitude as where you began. It can be slippery here, so let me suggest a few pointers to improve your footing. First, use the embedded stones and small logs as steps. Second, turn your feet sideways. If you slip with one, you should be able to hold on with the other. Third, take smaller steps to give yourself greater control.

At the bottom, the sandy path turns to the right to lead you more than half a mile parallel to the creek. It is a different feeling down here now that you've entered the riparian zone. You can hear the rushing water to your left, but it is best to wait before seeking it out. In the morning or evening, you might notice a pair of great blue herons flying by, as well as some birds of prey that like it around here. The leafy trees are cottonwood (rough dark bark) and sycamore (smooth white bark), along with alder (smooth dark bark). A few minutes ahead, it's still hard to resist jumping across to the creek as you pass a stone on your right I call "Putty Rock," a boulder that looks like "silly putty" for a giant-sized child.

It's only after 12 minutes on the canyon floor that you'll find your best chances to connect with the creek. You'll pass a bunch of tempting sand pathways on the left, but wait until you arrive at the flat, sandy part of this "inner gorge." The stones are colorful here, red and blond sandstone and blue-black basalt. Midgely Bridge is clearly in view by this point, and it actually feels as if you are pulling away from the creek. Up on the right end of the bridge is a parking lot, and visitors there are making their way to the viewpoint below. They're watching you, enviously.

Knowing that this is as good as it gets may be why highway worker Jim Huckaby built his little home here that he lived in during the second half of the 1930s. The trail today bears his name. A small weir is on the right, although I can't figure out where the water came from. It's about 30 feet further where you'll make your water choices. To the left you can skip over the rocks to the water slide, or you can stay right to follow the trail to a major water crossing.

You can take that side path over to the creek. If it's a hot, sunny afternoon, you'll see a bunch of sunbathers on the other side. But be sure to finish walking the main trail, which still holds at least one surprise. To do so, bear right, and about 100 feet ahead you'll discover a beautiful spot. Here Oak Creek looks remarkably placid, serving as a mirror to reflect the dramatic cliffs and green leaves that frame it. Paradise!

The Bridge & the Island

I wish I could guarantee you a way across the creek, but ever since its inception this seems to be Huckaby's little surprise for us. No bridge,

then a bridge, then the bridge got washed away, then rocks across: you may find any of these. (F) This much seems likely—if you're adventurous you'll try to get across. The water is not deep, but can be forceful, and the river bed is not flat.

If you don't want to hang out with the teens at the beach, then keep your eyes open as you walk this island. A few minutes ahead, on the right, you'll have the chance to drop into my favorite skinny dippin' hole. You'll find it just shy of a small cascade of water, creating a deep pool. Enjoy!

If instead you continue on, you'll soon reach another delightful spot with another uncertain creek crossing. There should be a bridge, but if not, it is easy enough to skip across on the rocks. (G) Here there's cool shade from the trees on the other side. It's a place nobody would want to rush past.

The Return Route

Whether this is the end of your trail depends upon your plans and upon the presence of a footbridge. You've either got a car parked waiting for you, or you plan to hitch a ride if you cross the creek.

If you choose to head up to Midgely Bridge, expect a zig-zag climb of just over 200 feet. The trail is wide and well marked, rising to a viewpoint next to the bridge. The final portion of the trail leads you under the bridge to the parking lot. (H)

If you're going to make a roundtrip of this, then there's little need to make the climb. I'd suggest enjoying the cool water instead and returning at your leisure.

As Long as You're Here On your way, chances are you'll pass or come close to one of Sedona's better gear shops, Sedona Sports. It's a good place to find hiking shoes, sunglasses, water bottles, GPS devices and all the other goodies that make your adventure complete.

Once you're done, reward yourself at The Oak Creek Brewery and Grill in Tlaquepaque with their award-winning beers. If you prefer grapes to hops, head to Hyatt Piñon Pointe shops and galleries where you'll find The Art of Wine. For great margaritas and Mexican food, the Javelina Cantina, also in the Hillside Plaza, is an excellent choice.

Uptown Sedona

Hiking Time:
4 hours, 25 minutes
for the roundtrip.

Trail Length:
8 miles
for the roundtrip.

The suggested side trip on the Cow Pies Trail adds about 2 miles and takes about an hour.

Elevation Change:
1,090 feet up.
Trailhead is 4,481 feet and the trail ends at 5,571 feet.

Munds Wagon Trail

This is the kind of trail you'll want to take a long afternoon to savor.

YOU'RE GOING TO LOVE THIS TRAIL.
From start to finish, bottom to top, and yes,
even on the way back, you're going to love this
trail. Munds Wagon Trail offers close-up points of
interest and far-off views in one delightful walk. It
varies in terrain, rises in height and lifts you up above
it all to bring you views so awesome that even the
most jaded walker can't help but be impressed. This is
a path through time, as geologic eons, a century-old
road, and a brand new trail come together.

Less steep than Bear Mountain but a longer walk,
Munds Wagon Trail is the kind you'll want to take
a long afternoon to savor. It heads from High Desert
to High Country, with seasonal options for waterfalls,
slickrock, blossoming agaves or spectacular sunsets.
Assuming you have the time, the energy, and the
ability to ignore the occasional noise of SUVs out
on the road, there really is no decision about whether
or not to walk this trail. The only decision is when.

Did I mention that you're going to love this trail?

Driving Directions From Uptown or from West Sedona, turn south onto Hwy 179 at the "Y." Turn left onto Schnebly Hill Road after 0.3 mile, just across the bridge past the Center for the New Age on the left (and Tlaquepaque on the right). Coming from the south, Schnebly Hill Road is on the right, 0.25 mile beyond the Hillside Sedona shops and galleries as you head north. Follow Schnebly Hill Road until the pavement ends. The parking lot and trailhead will be on your left.

For a shorter hike, continue up the dirt road 0.7 mile (about five minutes) to a small parking area on the left.

Trail Notes

• There are "environmental" toilets at the trailhead parking lot, but none after that.
• In March and April you may see waterfalls in the washes.
• Open areas on the Cow Pies can be extremely windy during the afternoon. Sometimes the breeze is refreshing, but either way you're exposed, so be careful in the summertime.
• This area is chilly in winter.
• No sign with an official trail number is posted for Munds Wagon Trail or Cow Pies Trail.

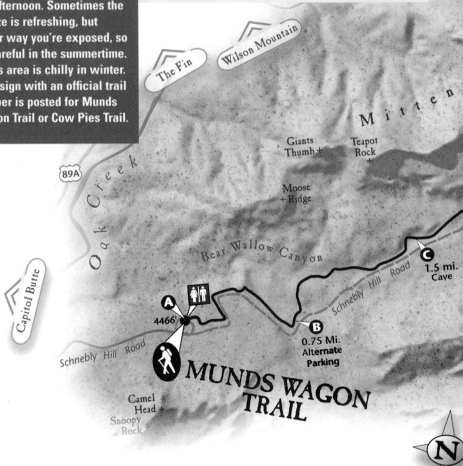

Munds Wagon Trail

Step 1, get to the correct trailhead. The one you want faces east, away from town. (A) Ignore the one by the larger ramada on the west side of the parking lot, which leads to the Huckaby Trail. Step 2, enjoy! For approximately the next two and a half hours you will be hiking up higher and higher as the views get better and better.

Through the High Desert

The trail heads down and to the right immediately, then curves back as you wind around a wide red rock basin. It is easy to imagine this basin in a rainstorm, when water pours over it. It's a gentle start that winds back to the left and then uphill, where you'll cross the dirt road by the large boulders. Here, glance back to see the city, and north to catch your last view of Sedona's highest peak, Wilson Mountain. By this point on the road most cars have long since turned around, a fact that may bring a smile to your face. Although you are about to cross the road for the first time and will cross it several more times before you are done, it's worth knowing that you will be seeing much more than will those behind the wheel.

This crossing heads east, across the road to an uphill entry back onto the trail. It's only a few minutes across this patch, which eventually curves left to come back down and cross the road again. You could choose to simply walk up the road, looking for the trail on the left...but then you came here for a hike, didn't you? So when you come back down onto the road, note that the trail on the far side drops off and isn't obvious.

Flying Buttress Ridge

5836'

928'

Cowpies

Munds Mountain

Upper Trailhead
4.0 Mi.
(G)
5597'

Merry
go-round
Rock

(E)
2.7 mi.
Road
Crossing

(F)
2.9 mi.
Cowpie
Junction

(D)
2.3 mi.
Toad Pool

Look for the brown stick with "trail" written on it in white. Now, as the trail winds down below the roadside, you really begin to feel like you're in the great outdoors.

The winding trail continues, further down and moving away from the road. To your right you'll pass a small parking lot, an alternate start and finish point for this hike (0.7 mile, 5 minutes of driving). Ⓑ As you move away from that lot, a photogenic spot appears. You'll be staring straight ahead at a great formation: Giant's Thumb. The spike of rock behind it is as interesting as the knobby thumb itself. As you get higher and closer to the perfect photo spot, the trail turns again to the right and again drops down.

With all this dropping, you're probably wondering when the climbing will start. In fact, it's a nice aspect of the trail that it deceives you in this way. First, you've already been climbing, but the views

HOW OUR TOWN GOT ITS NAME

Ellsworth Schnebly, arriving from Missouri to red rock country in the 1890s, soon wrote to his brother inviting him to join his farming venture. T. Carl headed down to check out the idea and when he decided the place looked suitable, he sent word to his young wife to bring her things.

That woman was the well-educated daughter of a wealthy Missouri landowner. He objected to the idea of his daughter, a woman "of high moral character," heading for the outlaw territory of Arizona. In fact, he threatened that if she went, he would take her out of his will. Ignoring the threat, which he followed through with, she soon joined her husband.

The Schnebly brothers decided the little town now needed a post office. T. Carl wrote to the U.S. Postal Service, which asked him to choose a suitable name. After submitting "Schnebly Station," he was told to be more succinct. Ellsworth quickly came to the rescue and suggested naming the town after T. Carl's wife. He liked the idea, and submitted "Sedona," his wife's first name, to an obliging Postal Service in 1902.

have distracted you from recognizing it. Moving farther away from the road, you'll feel a nice sense of solitude here.

What to do if you're on the trail when cars are heading back and forth along the road? First, ignore them. Second, have pity on them. From any point on the trail, you're seeing something they are missing.

Good views tower above you, so stop and take a look around once in a while. As you walk, you get a sense of the broadness of Sedona's terrain. Near the streambed you come to areas that may have a trickle of water running through. Though rare, a powerful flow of water here creates quite a sight. Above and to the south (looking in the direction of the road), Munds Mountain projects gray-white sandstone cliffs, sprinkled with evergreens, reminiscent of Zion National Park or even Yosemite. To the right, the bright orange-red cliffs are even more sheer, and it makes me think of another great park, Bryce Canyon. As you proceed, it is these red faces that will become more impressive.

Rounding behind the dry waterfall, you'll come into the forest and notice a park bench. It's a nice place to rest if you need it, but remember, the best is still to come! A few minutes ahead you'll encounter a cave-like red rock formation, and you'll feel blessed if you're able to see this when there's some water here. There's another small parking area here, serving as a better starting point (1.3 miles on the road from the trailhead; about 12 minutes of driving) if you have less time and are willing to move closer to the uphill portions.

The trail rises, keeping you to the left of the streambed, on a long, rolling portion that seems a little less interesting until you look up. High above and to the left, the red rock cliffs are more imposing than ever. The solid black streaks are clear evidence of water washing down, not eroding the rock but staining it. A tenth of a mile further you come to what I call "Three Falls Chute," where from the right angle you can see several flows in the creek bed. When you reach the last of the three, you'll drop down and cross the dry rock to enter the forest. Before you do, take a step out to the right, toward the road, to observe the puddles and colorations in the rock.

One of my favorite portions is coming up. Taking another left-to-right crossing, and look for the pipeline to the right under the road. Here a gentle laddering of the sandstone bed has created an effect that seems too perfect to be natural. One hundred paces ahead, the trail rises up to show you "Sinagua Paradise," my name for the horseshoe waterfall to the right. The last of the water thrills comes as you arrive at a wider, open area. Here you stand on flat red rock at the same level as the water. As you cross it, look upstream and see geological forces in action. Ⓒ Seen from above, the narrow chute is an obvious example of the erosion that quickly sculpts the sandstone. Toads and butterflies like it here too, and there are some good spots at the top of the chute to sit and relax. This is a good point at which to check the time, your water supply, and your energy level.

Up to the High Country

The route is about to rise, first up red rock itself and then, zigging and zagging, up a typical dirt trail. Reaching the high places, you enter Part II of the adventure: the High Country. Here the views are broad, never-ending, changing every few yards. It's several minutes more through forest before the trail comes to another road crossing. Ⓓ

Continuing on the main trail, it's about two-tenths of a mile uphill before another road crossing. On the other side of the crossing, the trail continues uphill at the same angle, heading right, and bringing the tall, gray sandstone cliffs into your vision. The highest peak is Munds Mountain, with an elevation of 6,834 feet. Once the trail turns back to the left, you'll be walking on red rock as much as on dirt.

This view features one of Sedona's most interesting and scenic formations. Ironically, it isn't what's on top of Merry-Go-Round Rock that is most fascinating, but what's underneath. The gray-white formation known as the Fort Apache layer is limestone formed by the organic materials of long passed-on sea life. As you climb higher, look for photo ops where it contrasts with the red rock.

One that I prefer comes just after you cross the streambed and arrive at a cairn with "Munds Trail" marked on the sign. Pass by this cairn, look for the next cairn after it, then turn left to photograph a curious hole in the Fort Apache layer. Alternatively, you can turn back and step off the trail, climbing to the left of the streambed if you want to get to the top of this formation. But most people will instead continue to what I call "Picture Frame Point," where you can take a nice seat and let your legs hang over this unique layer of rock. Here, the beautiful Schnebly Hill Formation is all around you.

I think this makes the best turnaround point, especially if you've walked all the way from the trailhead.

However, there is more climbing to do if you want the exercise and, of course, more views. The trail points directly uphill here, without a zig-zag. As you walk, a window emerges in the red rock pillars. Next to it is a narrow ridge I call "Little Indians," but which you may also hear called "The Tribe," or even better, "The Cocktail Party." After 10 minutes of walking, you'll rejoin the road. Take 25 diagonal paces to the left and you'll see a yellow road sign and a small trail sign. "Trail #58 – Schnebly Hill" begins here, climbing the original road up to the top of Munds Mountain.

I don't recommend Schnebly Hill Trail. The trail is a long, exposed slog, occasionally re-routed over rock slides. I've wondered if there is some maximum angle at which cattle, or wagon-pulling oxen, will move. That's what it feels like heading to the top of this trail. There is a brief change of scenery as the trail passes through a forested realm, with the ground turning to rich dirt and pine needles.

Instead, I recommend proceeding up the road. There you'll find a kiosk and a parking lot, past which a new view opens up of Wilson Mountain, Sedona's highest peak, with tiny Hwy 89A down at its feet. Ⓕ The lava flows that cap it are clearly visible, especially on The Bench, a shelf that stands out two-thirds of the way up. Look behind you and along the road and you'll notice that this layer of ancient lava—called *basalt* by geologists—is the level you've reached as well.

The Return Route

You'll enjoy marvelous views on the downhill. For more fun, head right at the signpost that says "Schnebly Hill Road." Ⓔ It takes you to the parking lot for the **Cow Pies Trail**, which is across the road.

Walking Cow Pies means contending with a bit of gravel at first, but the rewards are worth it. After 10 minutes, the trail curves left to reach "The Moon," my name for a red rock ridge speckled with basalt stones. The view is great.

It gets even better if you continue around on the Cow Pies Trail, eventually reaching another open red rock zone a further 10 minutes in. Here the main trail continues following small cairns up the red ridges on their right side. However, I recommend a sharp left turn along the current ridge. Before you turn, look northeast to see the window in the rock. Do you notice the turkey outlined by the rock to its left?

Heading left, the trail will invite you to climb up and over to the "cow pies" it is named for. Sometime late in the 20th century, a friend and I hiked here for the first time. When we returned home, we flipped on the television to see that NASA was about to send back the first photos from the Mars Lander. In the dramatic pause as we waited to see the photos, my friend leaned over to me and said, "I bet it looks just like Sedona." The pictures came on and looked so much like where we had been that we laughed the rest of the afternoon. If you make it out this far, I welcome you to the spot I now refer to as "Mars."

Your hike out retraces the Cow Pies Trail, as there aren't any safe, secure ways downhill. From there, cross through the parking lot to connect with the trail, or walk a few minutes down the road to re-enter it on the right hand side.

As Long as You're Here The proximity to town gives you a number of options for side trips before and after this hike. Before you go, stop in at Sedona Sports, an excellent source for hiking boots, walking sticks, caps, water and hydration packs, GPS equipment and more.

Once you're done with the hike, the Oak Creek Brewery & Grill in Tlaquepaque is a nice place to reward yourself. There's fine shopping and relaxing to be done in the stores and patios of this pleasant area. You can eat and drink well at El Rincon, The Secret Garden Café, Oak Creek Brewery and René.

West Sedona

Hiking Time:
5 to 6 hours
for the roundtrip.

Trail Length:
5 miles
for the roundtrip.

Elevation Change:
1,803 feet up.
Trailhead is 4,613 feet,
with the big finish on top
at 6,453 feet.

Bear Mountain

**Interesting terrain changes
yield more and more
spectacular views.**

YOU WANT A BIG HIKE? Not a stroll, not a walk, but something that makes you know you're alive if only because sometimes it feels harder than death? Not something so puny that your heart beats no faster than when you sit on a couch? You're looking for a big workout, a challenge, a mountain to match your energy. Welcome to the Bear.

Bear Mountain is a great big hike with much of what makes hiking in Sedona great. There are hearty climbs over, along and through red rock ridges. It takes concentration, good health and reasonable trail skills though, for there are more than a few opportunities to lose your way.

My question is always "Is it worth it?" The answer here is: "Absolutely!" Interesting terrain changes yield more and more spectacular views. If you've got plenty of time, health and ambition (and you're carrying plenty of water), take on this challenging hike.

Driving Directions Beginning at the "Y," drive 3 miles west on Hwy 89A to the stoplight at Dry Creek Road. Turn right onto Dry Creek Road, following it 2.8 miles until the stop sign. Turn left onto FR 152C for 1.5 miles until the next stop sign. Turn left following Boynton Pass Road/FR 152C, which is now a paved road. Follow this for 1.2 miles to the parking lot on the left and trailhead on the right. Driving time is 21 minutes from the "Y"; 32 minutes from the Village of Oak Creek.

Trail Notes

• There are no toilets here.
• Bring food and several quarts of water for each person.
• Ideal for spring and autumn. Bear's high elevation means problems during the extremes of summer (when there's little shade to be found) and winter (when there can be snow or ice on top).
• Very healthy types who know how to follow cairns can do this trail in 4 hours.
• Check the sunset time before setting out. Assuming you plan to go to the top, leave yourself five to six hours of daylight. This hike is not one to start late in the day, because you'll never be able to stick to the trail once it starts to get dark.
• Official name: BEAR MOUNTAIN, #54.

Bear Mountain Trail

Don't be deceived: Bear is bigger than it looks. From the trailhead, your eyes gaze up to the red rock formation above and you think, "Big, but I can do it." Sorry, Charlie. Bear is three times as high as this, and a whole lot farther away. Before you are done, you'll be looking down on this formation as if it were an anthill at your toes.

Think of Bear as having several plateaus, each of which offers a new challenge and rewarding views. Any one of them would be fine to stop at and end your journey, but I'm going to assume you want to make it to the top. So keep these tips in mind: stick to the main trail, avoid distraction and follow me.

Pass through the gate at the parking area to head toward the mountain. Ⓐ Within five minutes, you'll drop down through a pair of drainage ditches (called *arroyos* in the Southwest). The trail soon brings you to the trail register. Make absolutely certain to sign in.

Within the next few minutes you'll cross a grassland that should show you some wildflowers. As you walk, you can consider how to pace yourself for the climb, how in shape (or out of shape) you are and whether you really have enough time, food and water for the climb. Soon enough, you'll find out.

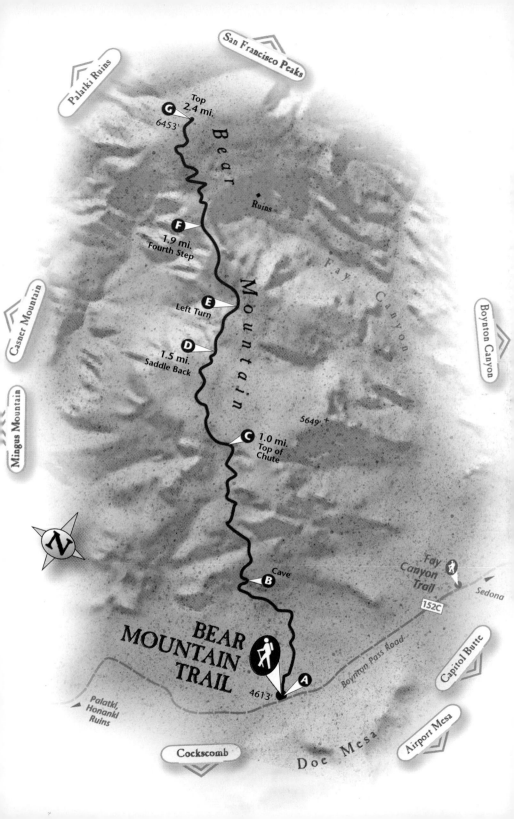

To the First Step

The first move uphill begins as you turn to the northeast for a 200-foot ascent. Pause to catch your breath as you face a cave-like indentation in the sandstone, and make sure to turn left. Ⓑ This takes you up the first chute, and there's much more climbing to come.

At the top of the chute is the first of many opportunities to be misled. You see, most people never make it to the top of the mountain. Whether through mistake or misfortune, they divert from the main trail. Likewise, at the top of the chute a weak trail heads left to an overlook. Bypass this overlook and you'll be rewarded by better ones ahead.

After a few more minutes of closely following small cairns you'll feel the trail flatten out. At this point, a substantial ridge towers to the north, with a tower of red rock to the east (to the right as you

SEDONA'S FAVORITE BEAR

Back in the days of Sedona's settler families, one man stood tall in both real life and legend. Jessie Jefferson "Bear" Howard of California got into trouble in the late 1870s for killing a herder whose sheep had grazed his land. Upon turning himself in, Howard was thrown into jail.

Legend has it that he escaped with the help of a hackblade baked in a cake, and made his way to the place where all outlaws of the era headed: Arizona territory. Arriving in Oak Creek Canyon in 1879 on the run from the law, he made his home near West Fork.

It is hard to tell which was taller: the enormous man's height or the tales later told of him. The stories include killing bears with nothing more than his knife; of his children being kidnapped by Indians; of a second prison escape; and beating up a man for mistreating a lady.

Although this mountain isn't named for him, you might call upon a dose of Bear Howard's energy and gumption to make it to the top.

face the ridge). It is natural to feel drawn to the tower, but the main trail heads in the other direction. A stump on the left side of the trail marks 5,071 feet and .62 miles, and the start of your turn west. ©

To the Second Step

Heading west, you'll walk for 15 minutes as the trail moves into a beautiful red rock bowl. Early on, make very sure to cross the dry streambed that cuts the trail. (Unlucky hikers tend to turn here, and not long ago it was full of cairns suggesting that that was what you should do.) Surveying the red rock walls, I love the fact that it is nearly impossible to tell where or how you'll be getting up. Just wait. The trail will climb up and step down a bit more vigorously now, until eventually it decides you're ready for an uphill stretch.

It's difficult to mark a starting point for the second chute, but I count it as a steep 160-foot gain in elevation. Is your heart pumping yet? If so, the rise above the chute will help only a little. This ridge is hardly flat, and there's another 160-foot rise to get to the summit of this one, although the grade is easier. Perhaps this is why Bear is such a good workout: the climbing is never over.

This ridge is full of distractions, with temptations to head way out to the left (east) or uphill over to the right (west). Instead, you'll follow the trail over the back of the ridge, being careful not to make the sharp right turn that takes you to a higher portion of the ridge. Keep your eyes straight ahead. Down in front of you is the trail, and up above now is the true summit of Bear Mountain.

The trail narrows as it drops down over the back of the ridge, then climbs up a hill. If Bear Mountain followed steps, then this would be Step 2. ⓓ You've now climbed over 1,000 feet in 1.75 miles. At the saddleback, it is the same old choice: dramatic overlook to the left, trail to the right. Fortunately, the overlooks and main trail grow closer as you continue to climb.

To the Third Step

Before you now, roughly in the direction of the summit, is the next ascent up the sandstone. This portion is both steep and tricky. As you climb, pause to look right to see the improving view of Fay Canyon below. Enjoy it a moment, then turn your full attention to the trail, looking for a left turn to take you up the steeper part.

The turn comes at 5,898 feet, 1.92 miles from the trailhead. This information is worthless without a GPS, of course, so rely instead on your eagle eyes to seek out small cairns leading the way to that left turn and to the rights and lefts that follow.

The saddle beyond the third step presents another dramatic western viewpoint. You'll know you're there when you see a lone juniper about 20 feet tall that stands above the dense manzanita.

To the Fourth Step

For once, it is okay to follow any of the small paths leading away from the overlook. Five minutes ahead you'll drop down a few steps. Now a narrow channel leads you alongside a checkerboard of sandstone and black lichen to your left. As you wind upwards and always to the left, Fay Canyon is a spectacular sight below. This is a great place to take a photo.

Another narrow chute brings you to the fourth step and to the numerically interesting altitude of 6,161 feet. I love this for a picnic spot, in spite of a small fire that broke out here in the summer of 2006. There are tall ponderosa pines here, and moving carefully, you can step out to overlooks facing south and west. Ⓕ

The Big Finish

The final portion of the trail moves up and forward, climbing rather steeply via a weak trail that alternates heading over sandstone and through low manzanita. The key turn comes 160 feet higher, about 10 minutes from the fourth step, as the trail reaches an exposed bit of sandstone. Here you'll turn left and begin a traverse heading west across Bear Mountain.

Like the knight moving forward on a chessboard, it's a few steps up and a few steps over. The narrow trail is a sign that not at all who come to this mountain make it this far. Watch for the trail to bring you to a pair of tall boulders embedded in the mountain. Your job is to hitch yourself up 10 feet or so to get over them, scrambling up the right-side rock.

Just as the ponderosa pine trees hint at a change in the plant life, the lack of sandstone cairns indicates new geology. Many of the rocks are colorful, yellow chert. Tough, rough stuff, it was occasionally used by native peoples for tools.

At the Top

Perhaps the only disappointment with the Bear Mountain trail is that there is no elegant finish. No signature book waiting up above, much less a bench to sit on. But chances are the views and the sheer joy of reaching the top will more than satisfy you. You'll know you're there when the narrow trail brings you to a fallen log. Cross it and continue 20 feet through the forest to the cliff edge. You've reached the summit at 6,453 feet, a distance 2.57 miles from the trailhead.

It is reward time. The first reward, of course, is that you made it. The second is to the north, where the snow-capped San Francisco Peaks of Flagstaff loom. Sacred to the Hopi and Navajo, they are over 12,000 feet tall and Arizona's highest mountains. Bear Mountain is one of the very few trails that give you a view of the Peaks from Sedona. Congratulations.

The dirt road below and to the west ends at Palatki Ruin, where the Sinagua resided for centuries. Both ruins and petroglyphs can be found there today. In the distance between Palatki and the Peaks is Bill Williams Mountain, located near the town of Williams, home of the Grand Canyon Railroad.

From here I recommend a small loop walk. Continue to the left and you'll get more views to the west and south. Walk carefully, as the edge is severe and look for brilliant orange Mexican Firedot lichen on the exposed stones. Closing the loop is a little tricky, and you'll probably have to step over a bit of yucca or squeeze through past some beargrass. Of course, you could just go back the way you came. Either way, don't panic. It might take a minute or two to find your way back, but you will. It's the only route around!

The lack of a picnic area up here makes the top of the fourth step a better place to "hang out." Though you'll lose the view of Red Canyon below and the Peaks in the distance, you'll gain a nice view looking out to the west. You'll see ranch land leading away from Sedona toward Cottonwood and Mingus Mountain.

The Return Route

A few things are worth noting for your downhill, which follows the same trail. First, take care with the steeper ascents. From the top, for example, I compare the walk to boulder hopping through a creek. You want to skip from rock to rock, because the loose dirt will drag you like rushing river water.

Two views are particularly prized. Now you'll see all the beauty of Fay Canyon at your feet. Further down, the return route through the second chute (from the second step down to the first) offers nice color on the red rocks as the sun sets to the west. These are both worthy photo stops.

As Long as You're Here On your way to Bear Mountain, I'd suggest a stop in town to pick up some grub for the trail. Three places I recommend are in the Old Marketplace Mall. New Frontiers sells sandwiches plus all of your juice, water and trail mix needs. Ravenheart, voted "best coffee" in Sedona, has coffee, teas and smoothies. New York Bagels, just around the corner, has great bagel sandwiches.

After the big hike, consider visiting nearby Palatki Ruin. Call 282-3854 for a reservation to see the site. Continue less than 3 miles on Boynton Pass Road/FR 152C, then turn right onto FR 795 for under 2 miles to reach Palatki. This is one of the few sites in the area where you can see both ancient dwellings and rock art.

GPS Data

The Global Positioning System (GPS) is a wonderful technological advance. Developed by the military, these devices use satellite telemetry to pinpoint any location around the world.

The GPS tables that follow coordinate with the letter-coded points (ie.: A, B, C) that appear on the individual trail maps and within the trail description text.

There are multiple ways to display GPS coordinates. This hiking book uses the "Hemisphere, degrees, minutes and decimal minutes" (H DDD MM.mmm) format and "WGS-84" datum, the default setting on most GPS devices.

Alvin Derouen utilized a *Garmin Rino* GPS to identify the latitude/longitude, elevation, and the distances from the trailhead for each GPS table.

BELL ROCK and COURTHOUSE LOOP (map pg. 17)

	Latitude	Longitude	Elevation	Distance
A	34° 47.485′	111° 45.693′	4,178 ft.	0.00 mi.
B	34° 47.858′	111° 45.779′	4,248 ft.	0.55 mi.
C	34° 48.178′	111° 46.014′	4,392 ft.	1.09 mi.
D	34° 48.321′	111° 45.705′	4,379 ft.	1.49 mi.
E	34° 48.387′	111° 45.081′	4,448 ft.	2.28 mi.
F	34° 47.971′	111° 44.860′	4,278 ft.	2.94 mi.
G	34° 47.850′	111° 45.448′	4,257 ft.	3.64 mi.

CATHEDRAL ROCK (map pg. 27)

	Latitude	Longitude	Elevation	Distance
A	34° 49.320′	111° 48.478′	4,050 ft.	0.00 mi.
B	34° 49.387′	111° 48.174′	3,995 ft.	0.40 mi.
C	34° 49.346′	111° 47.985′	4,002 ft.	0.53 mi.
D	34° 49.430′	111° 47.781′	3,999 ft.	0.80 mi.

BOYNTON CANYON (map pg. 45)

	Latitude	Longitude	Elevation	Distance
A	34° 54.460′	111° 50.942′	4,551 ft.	0.00 mi.
B	34° 55.176′	111° 51.261′	4,649 ft.	1.19 mi.
C	34° 55.544′	111° 52.106′	4,789 ft.	2.35 mi.
D	34° 55.418′	111° 52.685′	5,136 ft.	2.99 mi.
E	34° 55.419′	111° 52.685′	5,221 ft.	3.02 mi.

WEST FORK (map pg. 34)

	Latitude	Longitude	Elevation	Distance
A	34° 59.436′	111° 44.588′	5,260 ft.	0.00 mi.
B	34° 59.282′	111° 44.779′	5,256 ft.	0.32 mi.
C	34° 59.316′	111° 44.919′	5,238 ft.	0.78 mi.
D	34° 59.791′	111° 44.938′	5,238 ft.	1.23 mi.
E	34° 59.999′	111° 45.563′	5,313 ft.	2.2 mi.
F	n/a	n/a	5,480 ft.	3.2 mi.

DEVIL'S BRIDGE (map pg. 53)

	Latitude	Longitude	Elevation	Distance
A	34° 54.170′	111° 48.830′	4,598 ft.	0.00 mi.
B	34° 54.090′	111° 48.552′	4,655 ft.	0.35 mi.
C	34° 53.898′	111° 48.537′	4,855 ft.	0.65 mi.
D	34° 53.885′	111° 48.501′	4,882 ft.	0.70 mi.
E	34° 53.862′	111° 48.468′	4,881 ft.	0.74 mi.
F	34° 53.858′	111° 48.459′	4,959 ft.	0.84 mi.
G	34° 53.739′	111° 48.213′	4,960 ft.	1.12 mi.

DOE MESA (map pg. 59)

	Latitude	Longitude	Elevation	Distance
A	34° 53.620′	111° 51.926′	4,579 ft.	0.00 mi.
B	34° 53.604′	111° 51.920′	4,594 ft.	0.01 mi.
C	34° 53.420′	111° 51.878′	4,864 ft.	0.45 mi.
D	34° 53.499′	111° 51.663′	5,050 ft.	0.70 mi.
E	34° 53.523′	111° 51.567′	4,998 ft.	0.84 mi.
F	34° 53.506′	111° 51.523′	4,992 ft.	0.87 mi.
G	34° 53.470′	111° 51.498′	4,967 ft.	0.94 mi.
H	34° 53.404′	111° 51.421′	4,913 ft.	1.05 mi.

BRINS MESA (map pg. 61)

	Latitude	Longitude	Elevation	Distance
A	34° 53.272′	111° 46.096′	4,481 ft.	0.00 mi.
B	34° 53.440′	111° 46.220′	4,561 ft.	0.29 mi.
C	34° 53.834′	111° 46.503′	4,699 ft.	1.01 mi.
D	34° 53.892′	111° 46.548′	4,761 ft.	1.11 mi.
E	34° 54.017′	111° 46.762′	5,070 ft.	1.43 mi.
F	34° 54.100′	111° 46.645′	5,118 ft.	1.64 mi.
G	34° 54.454′	111° 46.440′	5,399 ft.	2.17 mi.
H	34° 54.509′	111° 46.375′	5,455 ft.	2.21 mi.

HUCKABY (map pg. 81)

	Latitude	Longitude	Elevation	Distance
A	34° 52.003′	111° 44.938′	4,448 ft.	0.00 mi.
B	34° 52.165′	111° 45.065′	4,411 ft.	0.72 mi.
C	34° 52.272′	111° 45.058′	4,508 ft.	0.87 mi.
D	34° 52.473′	111° 45.109′	4,506 ft.	1.31 mi.
E	34° 52.897′	111° 44.756′	4,321 ft.	2.03 mi.
F	34° 53.067′	111° 44.514′	4,311 ft.	2.38 mi.
G	34° 53.023′	111° 44.402′	4,310 ft.	2.46 mi
H	34° 53.141′	111° 44.496′	4,534 ft.	2.92 mi

MUNDS WAGON TRAIL (map pg. 91)

	Latitude	Longitude	Elevation	Distance
A	34° 52.002′	111° 45.821′	4,466 ft.	0.00 mi.
B	34° 51.949′	111° 44.461′	4,508 ft.	0.76 mi.
C	34° 52.182′	111° 43.897′	4,615 ft.	1.53 mi.
D	34° 52.265′	111° 43.236′	4,771 ft.	2.23 mi.
E	34° 52.298′	111° 42.948′	4,983 ft.	2.59 mi.
F	34° 52.286′	111° 42.769′	5,085 ft.	2.80 mi.
G	34° 52.934′	111° 42.667′	5,597 ft.	3.99 mi.

BEAR MOUNTAIN (map pg. 101)

	Latitude	Longitude	Elevation	Distance
A	34° 53.625′	111° 51.926′	4,613 ft.	0.00 mi.
B	34° 53.894′	111° 52.089′	4,834 ft.	0.46 mi.
C	34° 54.204′	111° 52.491′	5,533 ft.	1.07 mi.
D	34° 54.556′	111° 52.567′	5,671 ft.	1.75 mi.
E	34° 54.664′	111° 52.620′	5,898 ft.	1.92 mi.
F	34° 54.773′	111° 52.794′	6,161 ft.	2.20 mi.
G	34° 54.896′	111° 52.999′	6,453 ft.	2.66 mi

Note: All of the trail distances and elevations used in this book were derived from:
1. U.S. Forest Service published trail information.
2. USGS 7.5 minute topographic maps.
3. Survey measurements using a handheld GPS unit (Garmin "RINO 120")
At least two of the three sources had to be in agreement for a particular set of numbers to be included.

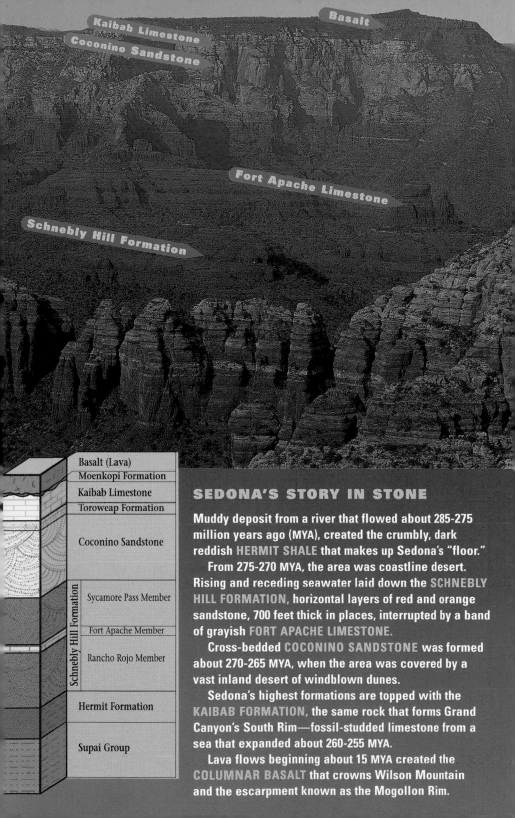

Basalt
Kaibab Limestone
Coconino Sandstone
Fort Apache Limestone
Schnebly Hill Formation

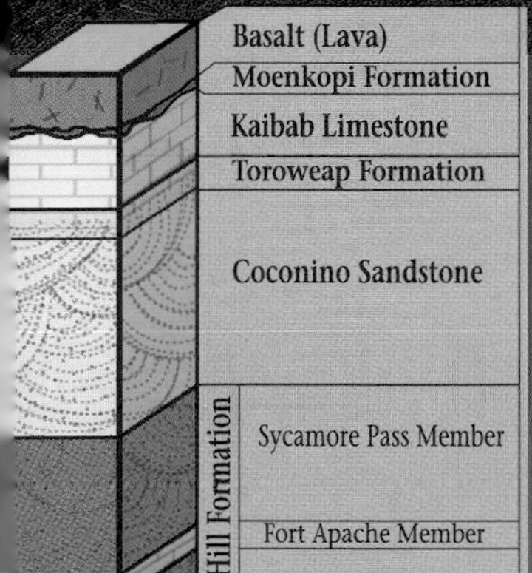
Basalt (Lava)
Moenkopi Formation
Kaibab Limestone
Toroweap Formation
Coconino Sandstone
Schnebly Hill Formation
Sycamore Pass Member
Fort Apache Member
Rancho Rojo Member
Hermit Formation
Supai Group

SEDONA'S STORY IN STONE

Muddy deposit from a river that flowed about 285-275 million years ago (MYA), created the crumbly, dark reddish HERMIT SHALE that makes up Sedona's "floor."

From 275-270 MYA, the area was coastline desert. Rising and receding seawater laid down the SCHNEBLY HILL FORMATION, horizontal layers of red and orange sandstone, 700 feet thick in places, interrupted by a band of grayish FORT APACHE LIMESTONE.

Cross-bedded COCONINO SANDSTONE was formed about 270-265 MYA, when the area was covered by a vast inland desert of windblown dunes.

Sedona's highest formations are topped with the KAIBAB FORMATION, the same rock that forms Grand Canyon's South Rim—fossil-studded limestone from a sea that expanded about 260-255 MYA.

Lava flows beginning about 15 MYA created the COLUMNAR BASALT that crowns Wilson Mountain and the escarpment known as the Mogollon Rim.

ABOUT THE AUTHOR

Dennis Andres is a writer, speaker, adventurer, and performer, drawing inspiration from his home among the red rocks of Sedona, Arizona. His humor, insight, and intellect have made him a popular commentator on Sedona for regional and national television. His company, **Sedona Private Guides**, specializes in creating personalized tours, hiking excursions, and spiritual adventures. He is the author of Sedona's best-selling books: *What Is A Vortex?*, *Sedona: The Essential Guidebook*, and the award-winning *Sedona's Top 10 Hikes*. Contact his office at 928-204-2201 for tour information or speaking engagements. Visit: www.MrSedona.com

ABOUT THE PHOTOGRAPHER

Larry Lindahl hikes and backpacks throughout the red rock canyons of Sedona, and is the author and photographer of the inspiring *Secret Sedona: Sacred Moments in the Landscape* (Arizona Highways Books). He captures landscape images with a medium-format film camera and his photographs have appeared on the covers of *Arizona Highways*, *Outdoor Photographer*, and many books. He also freelances for a variety of national publishers as an award-winning book designer. Visit: www.LarryLindahl.com

EXPLORE THE BEAUTY AND MAGIC OF SEDONA

Find out more about one of America's most beautiful places in these best-selling books.

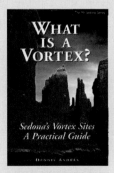 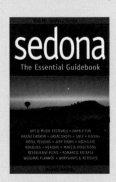 

What Is A Vortex?	*Sedona:*	*Sedona's Top 10 Hikes*
$8.95	*The Essential Guidebook*	$11.95
Practical guide to Sedona's vortex sites, places of unique energy for inquiring minds.	$16.95 Sedona's most comprehensive guidebook will help you to make the most of your visit.	Sedona's most in-depth, beautiful and descriptive hike book. An award-winning publication.

Dreams In Action Distribution
orders@DreamsInAction.us   www.DreamsInAction.us
(928) 204-1560   P.O. Box 1894, Sedona AZ 86339